Preface

Health is precious to everyone; yet promoting and protecting it is considered a cost to society. Children are precious to their families but still society tolerates the intolerable: child labour.

History tells us that when society is confronted with major social problems, a natural reaction is often to medicalize it. Health professionals cannot give a solution to social problems but should indicate an approach and show what can be done from a health perspective. They can alleviate the consequences but should not help in covering up the problem. They have a duty to care but also to denounce and alert.

This publication provides information on hazardous occupations so that priorities can be set by the legislators, policy-makers and authorities at national, municipal and community levels, including traditional leaders.

The main feature of this publication is to propose a strategy from a health perspective to address the problem of child labour. It identifies a possible model which may be of interest to a broad audience, including labour inspectors, health promoters and physicians, employers' and workers' organizations, local communities and advocacy groups. As a model, it requires an adaptation to local conditions, situations and needs, and must be tested in order to be validated and improved.

This publication was prepared by the Occupational Safety and Health Branch of the International Labour Office (ILO), based on experience gained since the ILO's Interdepartmental Project on Child Labour was launched in 1992. The financial contribution from the ILO International Programme on the Elimination of Child Labour (IPEC) made this publication possible.

J. Takala,
Chief,
Occupational Safety and Health Branch

Contents

Contents

Tables

I: Children's health and hazardous work

1. Introduction

Child labour remains a widespread and growing phenomenon in today's world. Many children worldwide work in extremely dangerous situations and in exploitative and abusive conditions. The types of hazards children face vary according to the occupation involved and the specific working conditions. The nature and extent of child labour, its forms and the severity of its exploitation, vary from one region to another and according to the country.

Some of the underlying causes of child labour are poverty, insufficient or unbalanced economic growth and in some cases structural adjustment policies. Without more equitable income distribution and general adult access to employment, and as long as economic growth is seen in terms of a higher gross national product, the problem will remain. Poverty is not the only reason for the existence of child labour. Deficiencies in the educational system, inadequate regulations to restrict child labour, ineffective enforcement of relevant legislation and lack of public awareness are also contributing factors. In developing countries, economic stagnation and unemployment, massive rural migration and accelerated urban growth, aggravated by the rising cost of living, have increased poverty and therefore the occurrence of child labour. In industrialized countries, where there is economic recession and unemployment has risen, certain forms of child labour have re-emerged.[1] There is increasing concern that the recent structural changes in Central and Eastern Europe are contributing to the extension of child labour in those countries as well.

Child labour has been mainly dealt with from a political, sociological and economic perspective. Much has been written and debated concerning the rights and well-being of children and their need for protection. However, little information is available concerning the actual conditions under which these children work and about the impact on their health.

In order to contribute to filling the gap of information on the health status of working children, the first part of the book provides an assessment of available information and discusses existing legislation, statistics, case-studies and other sources of information, on children's actual working conditions in selected occupations and their impact on children's health.

The second part of the book deals with a possible approach to the problem within a national policy for the elimination of child labour. In this context, it discusses the development of a programme on occupational safety and health to address working children.

The annexes provide an insight into technical instruments and their application to the evaluation of the damage caused to the physical and mental health of children in various kinds of jobs. They examine existing methodological tools on occupational safety and health and primary health care, which could be adapted to address the health status of working children for preventive and control purposes.

2. Current legislation and child labour

Concern about the health of working children led to the earliest child labour legislation and underlines most of the current legislation governing the employment of children. Almost all countries have incorporated the principle of prohibition of child work in hazardous conditions and activities in their national legislation, or define the conditions under which children may work. Despite the fact that concern about the health hazards faced by working children provided the impetus behind most of the current legislation regulating child labour, there is a wide gap between law and practice. Only a few member States have achieved full compliance with all the requirements, and there is an absence of effective measures to enforce this legislation. In some countries, there is still a lack of awareness of the need to protect the health and safety of working children.

A large number of countries have adopted legislation which excludes certain sectors or branches of economic activity (e.g. agriculture and work in plantations) and certain categories of workers (e.g. family enterprises and domestic services). Regulations frequently apply only to those persons who are under a contract of employment. Under these circumstances, a great proportion of the economically active population remains unprotected — in particular, child workers — because the kind of work which they perform most frequently is found in agriculture and the informal sector (e.g. children engaged in domestic work, in street trades and other self-employed activities). Indirect forms of employment in family trades, or in the production of goods through homework or on a piecework basis, are also excluded. As children are not supposed to be employed, there is no legislation protecting them even from the most dangerous and arduous work.

Another problem concerns the discrepancies which exist in many countries between the minimum age required by the law to work and that required to leave the school system. In several cases, the minimum age of admission to employment is lower than the school-leaving age, giving children access to employment before they have completed the minimum number of years of schooling. If children from impoverished families are legally allowed to work, they will do so and will drop out of school. However, the opposite situation also poses a problem, because if the minimum age of admission to employment is higher than the school-leaving age, children who leave school at the permitted age must wait one or more years before they are allowed to work. There is therefore a need to ensure that national labour and education laws are consistent, as called for in the Minimum Age Convention, 1973 (No. 138).

Most of the legislation pertaining to child labour falls into three categories. The first establishes a basic minimum age at which children may be employed and regulates permissible hours of work for children of various ages, sometimes differentiating between periods of the year when school is in session and when it is not. Such laws usually specify: the maximum number of hours a child may work per day and per week, relevant prohibitions concerning night work, the number of days of rest required per week and any annual vacation to which the child worker is entitled.

The second category concerns laws regulating child labour indirectly by establishing compulsory schooling until a certain age. Such laws exist in a number of countries, though the degree to which they actually prevent child labour differs among nations.

The third category of legislation addressing child labour directly concerns health and safety, as it specifically prohibits dangerous work. Several countries have a general prohibition of dangerous work for children and young persons which is not accompanied by any further specifications, and few, if any, implementing provisions. On the other hand, other countries list some of the occupations and activities which they consider too hazardous for the work of children, and are therefore prohibited. In many cases, the provisions that are supposed to protect children's morals are limited to prohibitions on working in nightclubs and on exposure to pornography or on selling alcohol to them.

Most national laws and regulations include, as prohibited activities or occupations: underground and undersea work, work in construction sites, use of machinery in motion, manufacture and handling of hazardous substances and work in bars and nightclubs. For example, Australia, Belgium, Colombia and Sudan prohibit the employment of children in work involving the use of lead paint. Argentina, Chile, Denmark, Italy and the United Republic of Tanzania prohibit the employment of children under the age of 18 years in underground mines. In India child labour legislation covers factories, plantations and workshops where certain types of hazardous work in industrial processes are carried out. The Philippines provides a comprehensive list of occupations, processes and industries considered to be hazardous for children. It has to be acknowledged that remarkably little information exists to evaluate the effectiveness of existing legislation in protecting the health and safety of child workers. A review of current national legislation pertaining to minimum age, with detailed summaries of national legislation regulating the exclusion of children from employment in hazardous industries, has been published by the ILO.[2]

The progressive elimination of child labour and the protection of children from work which endangers their safety, health and morals is a fundamental principle of many ILO Conventions and Recommendations as well as of international instruments concerned with the welfare of children, such as the UN Declaration of the Rights of the Child, 1959, the ILO Minimum Age Convention, 1973 (No. 138), with its accompanying Recommendation (No. 146), and the ILO Resolution concerning the Progressive Elimination of Child Labour, (1979).

According to the ILO, the term "child labour" covers all economic activities carried out by persons of less than 15 years of age regardless of their occupational status (wage-earners, own-account workers, unpaid family workers, etc). However, it does not include household work performed by them in their parents' home, except where such work can be assimilated to an economic activity as, for example, when a child must devote his or her entire time to that work so that his or her parents can be employed outside the home and is therefore deprived of the possibility of going to school. Moreover, it would be wrong to infer from this definition that any work performed by children under the age of 15 is prohibited under international standards, which would be neither feasible nor desirable. The Minimum Age Convention, 1973 (No. 138), authorizes the employment of children from the age of 12 or 13 in certain types of work such as light work under certain conditions, and allows certain categories of employment or work and certain branches of economic activity to be excluded from its scope.[3]

The Minimum Age Convention pursues a national policy designed to ensure the effective abolition of child labour and to raise progressively the minimum age of admission to employment. The minimum age should not be less than the age of completion of compulsory schooling and in any case should not be less than 15 years of age. The minimum age set for employment or work must be linked to the nature of the work and therefore the Convention specifies that "the minimum age for admission to any type of employment or work which by its nature or the circumstances in which it is carried out is likely to jeopardize the health, safety and morals of young persons shall not be less than 18 years". A lower age of 16 years may be authorized if the worker is fully protected and has received specific training. As a matter of priority, the prohibition of children working in hazardous activities, especially for the youngest and most vulnerable children, is a policy objective of the ILO's approach.

Other ILO instruments have specific provisions to protect children and young persons against hazards in dangerous occupations in relation to night work, hazardous employment, the handling of heavy weights, medical examinations, education and vocational training such as the Radiation Protection Convention, 1960 (No. 115), the Maximum Weight Convention, 1967 (No. 127), the Benzene Convention, 1971 (No. 136), the White Lead (Painting) Convention, 1921 (No. 13), and the Night Work Convention, 1990 (No. 171).

3. Statistics and sources of information on the health of working children

According to recent experimental statistical surveys carried out by the ILO Bureau of Statistics, there are at least 120 million children between 5 and 14 years of age working full time in developing countries, where child labour predominates. This figure would increase to about 250 million if we include those in the same age group who work as a secondary activity. According to the surveys conducted by the ILO in Brazil, Colombia, Ecuador, Ghana, India, Indonesia, Senegal and Turkey in 1993-94, most working children not only worked but were also studying. An average of 25 per cent of children between the ages of 5 and 14 were engaged in some form of economic activity. It was the principal activity for one-third of them and a secondary activity for the remaining two-thirds.[4] Asia, which is the most densely populated region of the world, has about 61 per cent of working children, whereas Africa has 32 per cent and Latin America 7 per cent. However, in relative terms, it is Africa which has the highest incidence, with an average of 40 per cent of children between the ages of 5 and 14 engaged in some form of economic activity. In industrialized countries, although child labour is less common, the phenomenon is growing again in several places, particularly in East European countries in transition to a market economy. In Turkey, the only industrialized country to have recently conducted a national survey of child labour, 986,131 children (8.3 per cent) between the ages of 6 and 14 were economically active in 1994.[5]

Data on occupational injuries and work-related diseases

Official statistics contain very limited data on working children and the other sources of information available come from non-official studies and reports which are of varying quality and objectivity. The coverage also varies widely. There is extensive literature on urban street children but much less information about the working conditions and health of the far greater number of children employed in agriculture and domestic services. Only limited information is available on how different kinds of work affect children's health and development.

There are few studies on the effects of specific hazards for specific groups of children. However, not enough information is available on specific non-fatal injuries and short- and long-term toxic exposures, and their effects on children.[6] Data available on mortality rates are insufficient and only a few studies exist on the cohorts of employed children. Data on ergonomic risks and on the growth and development of working children are almost non-existent, as compared to the number of studies on the health, growth and development of infant and preschool children. However, there are some reports comparing the health status of working children with non-working schoolchildren, from the same socio-economic group and of non-working children who do not attend school.[7]

Most of the studies available do not provide specific information on exposure to agents and target organs, nor on the effects of exposure to hazardous substances (such as dust, heavy metals, solvents and pesticides) with which children are interacting. However, in the 1980s the World Health Organization undertook a number of pilot studies in developing countries which provided the first important step in the collection of relevant health information on child workers.[8] Some of these studies showed that children were working in manifestly hazardous industries such as glass manufacturing, construction, mining and quarrying. In the case of less hazardous occupations, in several cases, work was carried out in excessively hot, damp, dusty or insanitary conditions which favoured the transmission of communicable diseases. Some children, domestic servants for example, are particularly vulnerable because of their work situation, being at the mercy of their employers and invisible to the outside world.

4. Occupational hazards for working children in specific occupations and industries

Working children are found in many sectors carrying out different types of activities in various forms of work situations mainly in the rural and informal sectors. It is rare to find children working in enterprises in the organized sector. However, some of these enterprises may contribute indirectly to the recruitment of children though their practice of subcontracting certain activities to small informal workshops or homeworkers who make intensive use of child labour.

Experimental statistical surveys conducted by the ILO in 1993-94 showed that child labour is on average twice as high in rural areas as in urban areas. Nine out of ten working children in rural areas are engaged in agriculture or similar activities, whereas in urban areas they are concentrated mainly in trade and services, in particular in domestic help, and to a lesser extent in manufacturing. The great majority of working children are employed in the informal sector of the economy. More than three-quarters of working children are engaged in family enterprises. Wage-earning accounts for a small proportion of total child labour and there are often far more boys than girls. Most children are employed in branches of activity which supply essentially domestic consumption.[9] In many countries, while elder children work in the fields or on construction sites, smaller children and even babies frequently play alongside their mothers at the workplace.

Some children are in fact engaged in activities that involve only light and unpaid work, in family enterprises, or have to face family responsibilities looking after younger brothers and sisters while their parents are working. However, many other children may be wage-earners in small-scale enterprises, in occupations as varied as brick-making, food processing, handicrafts and carpet manufacturing; they can be found in the service sector in bars and restaurants; in the informal sector, scavenging and rag-picking in the dumpsites in big cities. They may be engaged as domestic servants in households. They may be self-employed, engaged in marginal economic activities in the streets and therefore might be exposed to drugs, violence, criminal activities and abuses which damage their moral and emotional development. In some cases, children are also working under bonded labour.

The relative distribution of children among occupations may vary from one country to another, and some types of employment may be uncommon and thus exist only in limited areas. However, in general terms, working children in most countries are concentrated mainly in:

(a) agriculture, including plantations;

(b) small factories, small enterprises, cottage industries, family trades and home work;

(c) the services sector including domestic service in households; and

(d) marginal productive activities within the informal sector.

Almost every working environment involves one or several health and safety hazards. Occupational hazards can have health consequences on all workers. Chemical, physical, biological and stress hazards are found in the workplace in combination, and their adverse effects are often not only cumulative but intensified (synergistic), causing occupational accidents and diseases.

Children differ biologically from adults in their anatomical, physiological, and psychological characteristics because of their process of growth and development.[10] These differences may make them more susceptible to occupational hazards at the workplace as compared to adult workers, and the health effects can be more devastating for them, causing irreversible damage to their physical and physiological development, including permanent disabilities, with serious consequences to their adult lives. Anything that increases children's exposure increases their health risks.

Even if children can be exposed to the same hazards as adult workers in the workplace, in many cases the conditions of work of children and of adult workers are not the same. It is possible that children may be more exposed to an occupational hazard than adult workers in the same trade according to the type of task they carry out. In many cases, children tend to be given the most menial jobs, which often involve cleaning up adult workers' tools, for example. In such occupations, they are exposed to the cleaning agents they use (often solvents, or strong alkalis). In addition, they are at risk of greater exposure to any hazardous waste used which has been left around and has accumulated, as there is a lack of supervision of their tasks. For example, apprentice mechanics are frequently asked to clean workpieces with the aid of solvents; similarly, apprentice carpenters are often instructed to apply wood impregnation products, to do small painting jobs (priming coats) and to handle various kinds of adhesives without any protective equipment or safety information and, as a result, they are exposed to a variety of toxic substances, the nature of which they are often unfamiliar with. Frequently, the outcome is the endangerment of children's health and safety.

The conditions under which these children work are common to most of the occupations, for example, poor sanitary conditions, inadequate or non-existent personal protective equipment, inappropriate workspace and installations, old machinery and inadequate equipment or instruments, physical strain, long hours of work and low wages. Children involved in hazardous employment are also exposed to toxic chemicals, dusts, fumes and gases, hazardous physical and biological agents and ergonomic hazards. Exposure limits are placed at adult levels and may not be respected anyway. Under such conditions children suffer from fatigue, aggravation of non-occupational diseases, and misdiagnosis of diseases attributed to non-occupational factors. They are premature victims of work-related diseases and incapacitation.

Table 1 provides some examples of hazards to which working children may be exposed, according to the main types of work in which they are actually engaged, for easy reference. It describes the types of industry or sector of activity, the tasks undertaken, the hazards they may face and the health consequences for working children. Some of the occupations are discussed in Annex II.

Occupational accidents

Occupational accidents are determined by the physical working environment, tools and equipment used to perform certain tasks that require careful operation and training. Safety hazards could provoke harm in an immediate and, in some cases, violent manner and can lead to injuries such as burns, cuts, electrical shocks, sprains, broken bones, loss of limbs, eyesight or hearing damage. The main sources of safety hazards are: fires and explosions, electrical appliances, dangerous stationary machines, special operations requiring eye protection (e.g. grinding metal or wood, use of liquid aerosols, spills and mists), moving and lifting equipment, noise, vibration and ergonomic factors.

Despite the fact that little data on work-related accidents of children is available, it is often found that children and young workers tend to

TABLE 1. EXAMPLES OF HAZARDOUS OCCUPATIONS AND THEIR CONSEQUENCES ON THE HEALTH OF WORKING CHILDREN

Enterprise/Industry/Sector	Tasks	Hazards	Health consequences
Agriculture	Working with agricultural tools and machinery; use of lawnmowers and circular saws; handling and spraying of agrochemicals; caring for farm animals and herding sheep; crop picking and weeding; collecting fodder; loading.	Inadequate or unprotected machinery and tools; driving tractors and farm vehicles; motor vehicle accidents; noise and vibration; risk of falls and suffocation in grain elevators and silos; dangerous animals, biological toxic agents; exposure to hazardous chemicals; arduous work; working without personal protective equipment; exposure to extreme temperatures; heavy loads.	Lacerations, cuts, injuries and death, fractures and amputations of fingers, limbs and toes, head injuries or other handicaps caused by equipment and farm machinery mishaps; induced hearing loss; eye injuries; parasitic infections and other infectious diseases; dermatitis; thermal stress; chemical poisoning (chronic and acute).
Mines (quarries and underground)	Carrying rocks, slate slabs or other heavy weights; digging and quarrying; bending over, kneeling or lying down in cramped positions in underground work.	Risk of falls; injuries due to falling objects and fatal accidents; risk of explosion from methane; exposure to harmful dusts, gas, fumes, carbon monoxide; strain from carrying heavy loads; arduous work; poor sanitation; inadequate nutrition; noise.	Fractures and injuries caused by falling objects; death; respiratory diseases (silicosis, pulmonary fibrosis, emphysema); physical strain and fatigue; musculo-skeletal disorders.

Construction work and brickmaking	Digging earth; carrying loads; shovelling sand and cement; metal work; roofing; working with wallboards and fixing pipes; crushing, grinding, screening and mixing clay in brickmaking; carrying bricks.	Injuries due to falls and falling objects; arduous tasks; exposure to harmful dusts and noise; exposure to asbestos; poor housekeeping; working without personal protective equipment; extreme weather conditions; silica exposure, carrying of heavy weights; lead exposure from glaze; excessive heat from ovens; carbon monoxide from kilns.	Musculo-skeletal disorders; respiratory diseases such as asbestosis; fatigue; injuries caused by falling objects and by stepping on sharp objects; falls from heights; burns; lead poisoning, silicosis, carbon monoxide intoxication; thermal stress.
Textile workshops	Spinning; weaving; knitting; finishing natural and synthetic fibres; dyeing, trimming.	Unsafe machinery; noise; inhalation of contaminated dust; exposure to man-made fibres, asbestos dust; poor lighting; exposure to chemicals; inadequate ventilation; high humidity; high temperatures; working without personal protective equipment; lifting and carrying of heavy loads; poor housekeeping; risk of fire.	Cuts and injuries from machines; chemical poisoning; respiratory lung diseases; induced hearing loss; musculo-skeletal disorders; byssinosis; asbestosis; physical strain.
Carpet-weaving workshops	Yarn preparation; wool sorting, washing, hand spinning and weaving, dyeing, trimming.	Inhalation of wool dust contaminated with biological agents; inadequate working postures (squatting); inadequate lighting; hazardous chemicals; inadequate ventilation, housekeeping and sanitation, repetitive movements.	Musculo-skeletal disorders; eye strain and defective vision; respiratory diseases; fatigue; chemical poisoning.

Enterprise/Industry/Sector	Tasks	Hazards	Health consequences
Garment and leather workshops, tanneries and footwear manufacture	Cutting and incision; chasing; moulding; embossing; hammering; mosaic formation; trimming; bonding; stitching; dyeing; sewing.	Inadequate ventilation; noise; exposure to glues and solvents; exposure to formaldehydes and dyes; blocked exit doors; accumulation of combustible materials; overcrowded workspaces; poor house-keeping; risk of fire; overloaded electrical supplies and exposed wires and fuse boxes; unsafe machinery and sharp instruments; working without personal protective equipment; shift work and long hours of work.	Cuts and injuries from machines and sharp instruments; burns; loss of fingers; fatigue, electrocutions; chemical poisoning; fire accidents; musculo-skeletal disorders.
Ceramics and glass factory work	Sorting and cutting glass; firing ceramics; colouring glass; drawing molten glass; carrying hot glass.	Radiant heat and thermal stress; stepping on or handling hot broken glass; poor ventilation; hazardous dust; exposure to lead.	Burns; cuts from broken glass; eye injuries; heat stress; respiratory diseases; lead poisoning.
Matches and fireworks workshops	Mixing hot chemicals; making matchsticks and boxes; stuffing cracker powder into fire crackers.	Exposure to hazardous chemicals; risk of fire and explosion.	Intoxications; burns; injuries and death by explosions.
Slate-making	Carrying slate slabs; colouring and polishing slates; fixing nails; cutting wood frames and frame fitting; packing.	Carrying heavy loads, exposure to silicious dusts and quartz dust from slate particles; noise exposure.	Silicosis, and other lung diseases, premature incapacitation.

14

Activity	Tasks	Exposure	Health effects
Paint shops	Painting and paint scraping.	Exposure to leaded paint, solvents, and other chemicals; inadequate ventilation.	Chemical poisoning, neurological impairment; musculo-skeletal disorders; dermatitis; lead poisoning.
Metalwork	Welding, soldering and smelting of metals (lead); brasswork, electroplating.	Exposure to extreme heat; flying sparks, exposure to lead and other hazardous metal vapours.	Eye injuries, thermal stress, burns, neurological impairment; lead poisoning.
Toymaking	Making toys with different types of raw materials including wood, metal, cotton, plastic, etc.	Exposure to solvents, dyes, paints, adhesives and metals for electroplating; use of sharp tools.	Burns, dermatitis, chemical poisoning, injuries, lead poisoning.
Buttonmaking	Autoclaving; sawing; pressing and punching bones, metal, wood, plastic; pulverizing, mixing and moulding horn and plastics.	Unguarded machinery, dust exposure, risk of fire or explosion, chemical exposure, noise, vibration.	Repetitive strain injuries; ocular fatigue; chemical poisoning; hearing impairments.
Abattoirs and meat processing, butcher shops	Slaughter of animals; cutting of carcasses; separating edible and inedible parts; removing hair and skin of dead animals; cleaning pens; carrying carcasses; use of water-heating vessels.	Unsafe machinery and equipment, exposure to biological agents, exposure to extreme temperature changes; poor sanitation, exposure to untreated liquid and solid waste; inadequate ventilation.	Injuries from falls; cuts and abrasions from sharp tools and mechanical saws; burns and scalds; Q fever; brucellosis; tuberculosis and other infectious diseases; thermal stress; eye injuries from flying bone splinters; physical strain; respiratory diseases.

Enterprise/Industry/Sector	Tasks	Hazards	Health consequences
Precious stones and gems industry	Gem polishing; gem carving; domestic work.	Inadequate ventilation; bad sitting postures; limited workspace; poor lighting; poor sanitation; exposure to chromic oxide, ferric oxide, silica.	Injuries from cutting disc blades; musculo-skeletal disorders; eye strain and defective vision; dermatosis and chemical poisoning; fatigue; silicosis; gastro-intestinal diseases.
Deep sea fishing (Muro-ami)	Diving to depths down to 60 metres to beat on coral reefs to scare fish into nets.	Exposure to high atmospheric pressure; accidents due to oxygen deficiency (hypoxia); exposure to carnivorous and poisonous fish (needlefish, sharks, barracuda snakes); overcrowaed and insanitary conditions and inadequate food on board vessels; long hours of work.	Decompression illness; death or injury from hypoxia; gastro-intestinal diseases; emphysema and cardiac disorders.
Dock work	Trimming and stocking, and other stevedore duties.	Lifting and carrying heavy loads; falls from heights; arduous work; poor housekeeping; exposure to heat; long hours of work.	Injuries from falls; burns; respiratory diseases, fatigue, physical stress and strain; musculo-skeletal disorders; thermal stress.
Services sector: Food services (restaurants, fast food shops, grocery stores, supermarkets, butchers' shops, bakers' shops)	Handling and serving food; stocking shelves, working as cashiers; cleaning ovens; manipulating and carrying cardboard boxes; stocking shelves.	Exposure to microwaves; electric hazards; exposure to extreme changes in temperature; slicing machines; unsafe use of ladders; carrying heavy loads.	Minor lacerations and burns; electrocution; thermal stress; amputation of fingers; injuries from falling objects; carpal tunnel syndrome; injuries from crushing machines; falls from ladders; and strain.

Auto repair garages/petrol stations	Repair of storage batteries; degreasing metals; electroplating; housekeeping; minor mechanical repairs; tyre maintenance; washing cars and fuelling tanks.	Exposure to carbon monoxide, benzene, solvents and asbestos; noise; unsafe tools and machines; manual handling of heavy objects; inadequate ventilation; poor housekeeping; risk of fire or explosion.	Burns, injuries, carbon monoxide poisoning; falls; hernia and strain; dermatitis; chemical poisoning (lead, burns, injuries, carbon monoxide); asbestosis; lead poisoning.
Entertainment (theatre, circus, bars, nightclubs)	Acting, modelling, performing in circus, serving.	Falls; long hours of work; night work; irregular meals; sexual and moral abuse.	Injuries, health effects of long working hours; mental stress and behavioural disorders.
Marginal productive activities: Domestic service/housework	All types of domestic work, including child care.	At the mercy of the master/mistress; long hours of work; lack of minimum facilities to sleep or rest; abuse of health and morals (sexual or physical abuse, demeaning work); isolation from society; irregular meals, corporal punishment.	Health effects of long hours of work and insufficient rest; malnutrition; psychological stress (from sexual abuse, confinement, fear of destitution); physical injury.
Home-based manufacture	Sewing, electronic assembly, jewellery making, etc.	Hazards depend on the type of work carried out; poor lighting and inadequate working conditions are frequent; environmental exposure, even if not working.	Fatigue from long hours of work in inadequate conditions and from hazards associated with the type of product.

Enterprise/Industry/Sector	Tasks	Hazards	Health consequences
Scavenging and rag-picking	Reclaiming usable material from garbage heaps.	Cuts from glass/metal; exposure to hazardous substances including waste from hospitals; inhaling stench from putrefied matter; infestations of flies; temptation to eat leftover food; insanitary conditions (water, food and shelter); risk of being run over by big trucks or bulldozers; living near the dumpsite.	Cuts, burns, tetanus; chemical poisoning; infectious diseases (HIV/AIDS, hepatitis, etc.); tuberculosis, respiratory diseases; food poisoning; malnutrition; injuries and death.
Prostitution	Sex with partners.	Exposure to drugs, violence, abuse, bondage, danger to health and morals; exclusion from family and community.	Sexually transmitted diseases (syphilis, hepatitis and AIDS); psychosocial disorders; unwanted pregnancy.
Street work	Hawking and vending goods; carrying drugs; selling newspapers; shoe polishing; begging; cleaning car windows; red-light performances; delivering goods; being messengers.	Exposure to drugs, violence and criminal activities and prostitution; exposure to traffic accidents, danger to health and morals.	Motor vehicle injuries; victims of drug addiction; branded as social outcasts (reconvicted criminals); long working hours, fatigue, malnutrition; AIDS and other sexually transmitted diseases; psychosocial disorders; unwanted pregnancy.

have more serious accidents than their seniors, although, here, much depends on the workplace, on the circumstances and on the extent of the restrictions placed on the employment of children.

According to the World Health Organization, injury is the first cause of death among children and adolescents and one child in every five or ten sustains an accident each year.[11] The most common injuries are: burns and scalds (in rural areas from firewood used for cooking on an open fire); falls (from trees when picking fruit, lack of protection on roofs and stairs and/lack of maintenance of protective devices); and poisoning (from accidental drinking of medicines and chemicals, particularly pesticides). Also frequent are animal bites (rabbits, dogs, cattle, poisonous snakes), drowning (in wells without protective barriers), traffic accidents and agricultural accidents with machinery.

Some types of accidents are liable to lead to severe injuries with the possibility of death or disability. Any fall from a significant height can cause severe head injury, internal or spinal injuries and limb fractures. Poisoning, drowning, burns, and scald injuries involving more than 15 per cent of the body surface in a child, account for the accidental deaths of many children.

Children starting work do not always perceive danger correctly, due to lack of information and experience, or else they have an impression of insecurity and vague danger, but may not always clearly perceive the relationship between an eventual outcome and the danger of a particular hazard, or they may come to the wrong conclusions. In some cases, they lack the experience to judge a situation correctly, anticipate what will happen and decide quickly what is to be done. When faced with a series of events which will inevitably result in an accident, or when an accident has taken place, they may not know how to behave. They are less likely to know what to do when accidents occur, and lack familiarity with the machines, tools and equipment they are expected to use. Most children blame themselves for the injuries they have and almost never complain to their parents or consult a doctor unless it is a serious accident. There are also other factors, e.g. competition among children to retain the job, lack of environmental and personal protection and poor sanitary conditions. A child worker has not yet mastered the most efficient, or the fastest and safest working techniques; his or her movements are not always well-controlled and in proportion with the desired result, and he or she may not receive appropriate training. A child is inclined to use makeshift tools, rather than having access to the proper ones or to appropriate protective equipment. Furthermore, if they are exposed to long hours or arduous work, fatigue will contribute to the occurrence of accidents.

Occupational diseases

Occupational diseases are caused by exposure to harmful agents (chemical, biological or physical) found in the workplace. Health hazards are often slow-acting, cumulative, irreversible and complicated by non-occupational factors (e.g. malnutrition). When the causal agent of the disease can be identified, measured and controlled, the initial health effects can often be reversible if the sick person is treated promptly.

When dealing with the health of child labourers, counteracting a certain disease often requires dealing simultaneously with more than one condition. Children may be predisposed to occupational diseases by poor health, characterized by malnutrition, anaemia, fatigue and debilitation from infectious and parasitic diseases, which interact with hazardous working conditions, inadequate or non-existent personal protective equipment, physical strain and a poor sanitary environment, making them more vulnerable to occupational diseases than adult workers. In the case of work-related impairments, the exposure to hazardous agents and inadequate working conditions has synergetic effects which exacerbate the already poor health status of those children and provoke a further deterioration of their health which can lead to permanent disabilities and premature death, e.g. malnutrition and tuberculosis associated with exposure to hazardous dust can result in pneumoconiosis in early adulthood.

As mentioned before, children's inexperience may expose them to additional risks as compared with adult workers in the same conditions.

They may not know how to carry out welding operations while avoiding the noxious fumes which are produced, or how to perform certain other tasks without unnecessarily producing great quantities of dust and thereby increasing exposure. For all the reasons outlined above, children's exposure to hazardous substances should be avoided.

Ergonomic hazards

Safety and health problems also arise because — as children are not supposed to be working for a salary — children's physical proportions, working capacity and limitations are not taken into consideration in designing work methods, tools and equipment. Therefore, they are more at risk of being injured. Children using hand tools designed for adults run a higher risk of fatigue and injury. When personal protective equipment does not fit children, they have to work without it or use alternative devices, such as handkerchiefs to cover their nose and mouth, which do not provide real protection. Children using seats and workbenches designed for adults may develop musculo-skeletal disorders such as chronic repetitive strain injuries, repetitive motion trauma (these are repetitive minor "insults" to a part of the body that develop only after a certain period of time), back problems, tenosynovitis, vibration-induced disorders and white finger syndrome.

In heavy work, including carrying of heavy loads, excessive stress may be placed on the bones before the epiphysis has fused and may result in skeletal damage or impaired growth because they are undergoing the process of growth and development. Identifying and eliminating risks related to work design would be particularly difficult in relation to children because their growth and development rates vary from individual to individual.

Heavy work at an early age also has other direct consequences on the child's physical and mental development. Physically, children are not suited to long hours of strenuous and monotonous work. Their bodies suffer the effects of fatigue due to excessive energy expenditure faster than adults, and most of these children also suffer from malnutrition due to inadequate food intake, which lowers their resistance and makes them more vulnerable to illnesses. The prevalence of anaemia, poor nutrition and long hours of work further reduces children's working capacity, and fatigue contributes to the frequency and severity of accidents and diseases.

Harmful substances and sources of exposure

Children's structural and functional characteristics differ from those of adults in terms of morphological, physiological, biochemical, metabolic and behavioural characteristics, as well as their nutritional requirements. The characteristics of an infant, a young child and an adolescent will differ during childhood. These variations represent stages in the normal growth and development of children, and their vulnerability in each stage may determine the different ways in which they are affected when exposed to hazardous agents and substances, particularly in the case of chemicals.

The toxic effects of a substance depend on the dose level of exposure, the length of exposure, the concentration of the substance, as well as other contributing factors, e.g. a special individual sensitivity to the substance. A health effect may be reversible or irreversible, depending on the regenerative capacity of the damaged organ or tissue.

Some of the biological characteristics of children when compared to adults are:

(a) rapid growth and development of the body as a whole and the organs and tissues, which are functionally immature at the time of birth and which become mature at different rates;

(b) different body composition;

(c) a larger surface area in relation to weight;

(d) a higher metabolic rate and oxygen consumption and therefore greater intake of air per unit body weight;

(e) greater energy and fluid requirements per unit body weight.

Rag-picker in the dump site of a big city (Photo: Jacques Maillard, ILO Photo Library)

Child exposed to the toxic vapours of solvents and varnish (Photo: Habibe Şentürk, ILO Photo Library)

Child working in a welding shop (Photo: Jacques Maillard, ILO Photo Library)

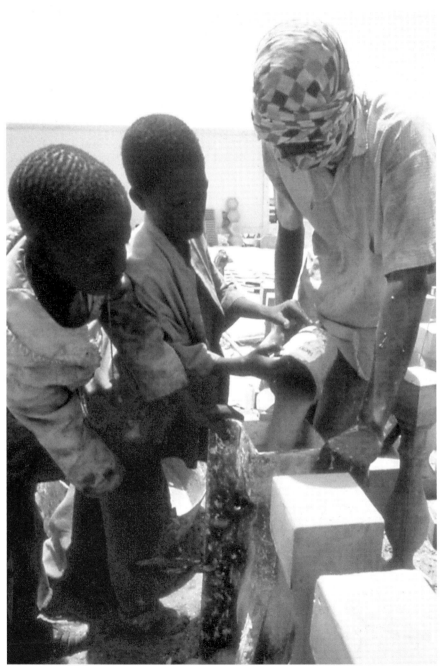

Children working in a brickyard (Photo: Jacques Maillard, ILO Photo Library)

Girl selecting tobacco leaves (Photo: Sabahattin Alaçam, ILO Photo Library)

Child working in a jute plantation (Photo: M. Schapira, ILO Photo Library)

The response of children to chemicals may differ from the response of adults because of the biological characteristics mentioned above. The effects of chemical exposure and chemical interaction may also vary with age. These effects can be greater or lesser than in adults depending on the chemical characteristics, their metabolization and the degree of maturation of target organs and tissues. The exposure, intake and effects of a chemical may be modified by factors concerning the mode of nutrition, the social, economic and cultural conditions, and health status.

There is limited information on the type, severity and outcome of the exposure of working children to toxic substances. Most data on toxicological effects of hazardous substances are based on animal laboratory studies and epidemiological studies of adult working populations. Some references are made in scientific literature to various occupational risks to which children and young persons appear to be particularly sensitive and to which it is generally agreed that growing children should not be exposed. However, due to lack of information on the dynamism of toxicity on children as compared to adults, some generalizations based on "common sense" have been made concerning the potential harmful effects of toxic substances on children, which in the light of new research have been shown to be inconsistent. For example, it has been suggested that the thinner dermis and epidermis of children allow an increased absorption of dangerous chemicals.[12] However according to recent studies, there is no significant difference between the thickness of the epidermis of a child and an adult, even though a child's dermis is structurally a little thinner than that of an adult. Therefore, the characteristics of a child's skin do not necessarily contribute to a greater risk of intoxication than in an adult's skin.[13]

The toxic effect of brief exposure to a high concentration is different from prolonged exposure to a low concentration. Prolonged exposure to different toxic substances even in low concentrations may cause a diversity of toxic effects. Neural-behavioural functional changes can be early indicators of prolonged exposure to toxic substances at low concentrations. Other effects may be hepatic, renal, skin, pulmonary or reproductive impairments. Children have a longer period of exposure to cumulative hazards if they start working at an early age.

Working children may also be exposed to a toxic substance for a longer period of time than adults. The exposure to substances with long latency periods during early life, such as asbestos, would increase the possibility of contracting chronic occupational diseases such as lung cancer, in young adulthood instead of at an older age. Some authors have raised concern about the exposure to toxic chemicals at a very young age, which may alter the body response to future toxic exposures.[14] For a more extensive discussion on chemical exposure, see Annex III.

Exposure to physical agents

Children have a lower heat tolerance than adults and, therefore, are subject to a higher risk of heat stress at work. For this reason, maximum permitted heat levels for adults may not be stringent enough for children. Heat stress is greater in children because their sweat glands are developing and the same moderately low environmental temperature will cause an increase in the consumption of oxygen of the child before that of the adult. As the child grows and becomes more active, muscular activity plays a more important part than temperature in oxygen consumption.

In studies on noise exposure among young and adult workers, it has been found that young workers are more susceptible to induced hearing loss than adults. Noise exposure limits set for adults would not be adequate for children. Ionizing radiation is likely to be particularly harmful for children, since its injurious effects on growing tissues are well known and the risk is cumulative i.e. the sooner the exposure starts the higher the lifetime dose which could be reached.

Table 2 provides information on the hazardous physical, chemical and biological agents to which working children may be exposed, according to the sources of exposure and type of health consequence. It describes the type of industry, process or activity in which these hazardous agents can be found, and the diseases and health consequences that they can cause. Some of the most hazardous agents are discussed in Annex III.

TABLE 2. OCCUPATIONAL DISEASES AND OTHER HEALTH IMPAIRMENTS CAUSED BY PHYSICAL, BIOLOGICAL AND CHEMICAL AGENTS

Hazardous agents	Sources of exposure	Health impairments
Biological agents:		
Contact with bacteria or virus through contact with domestic and wild animals	Abattoirs, working with agricultural animals, bone and meat processing, butchers' shops, ivory and horn processing, poultry, stock farming, tanneries	Anthrax, brucellosis, catarrh, dermatitis (erysipeloid), herpes virus infections, hepatitis, Q fever, leptospirosis, rabies, rat-bite fever, ringworm, salmonellosis, toxoplasmosis, tuberculosis, asthma
Cotton, flax, linen	Mixing and card rooms, rope-making, soft hemp, textiles, twine making, ball-pressing plants, ginneries	Byssinosis
Dry bagasse of sugar cane stalks	Building materials (insulating wallboard, fillers for veneered doors), cardboard, chemically treated press boards, explosives, fertilizers, paper, fuel, poultry feed, refractory bricks	Bagassosis
Physical agents:		
Work in compressed air	Deep-sea diving	Decompression sickness
Ionizing radiation and radioactive substances (children are rarely exposed to them)	Radium-dial painting; uranium mining; use, analysis or manufacture of radioactive materials	Teratogenic and mutagenic effects, leukaemia and other forms of cancer

Hazardous agents	Sources of exposure	Health impairments
Infra-red radiation	Arc processes, hot furnaces, molten glass, molten metals, presence of infra-red radiation	Cataracts
Noise	Textile engineering works, boilers, explosives, compressors, etc.	Hearing impairments
Other physical agents (cold, heat, humidity, sunlight, ultraviolet rays, electricity, high energy sources such as X-rays)	Electric furnaces, metal-burning, molten metal pouring, pipeline work, plasma torch burning, welding, contact with liquid tar, dyes (those activated by light)	Dermatitis and other skin diseases
Chemical agents (including metals):		
Chemical agents (cleaners, plastics, solvents, acids, detergents, inks, pesticides, soaps, peroxides, abrasives, cement, dyes, chromium, epoxy resins, formaldehyde, fungicides, mercury and cobalt salts, nickel)	Construction, cleaning, bakeries, electroplating, leather, metal, paint, printing, rubber, textiles	Dermatitis and other skin diseases including eczematous lesions
Lead and its toxic compounds (organic, inorganic, lead tetraethyl)	Ceramics, insecticides, lead lining, smelting, printing presses, storage batteries, brass-work, paint and paint scraping, stained glass, gasoline fuel for internal combustion engines	Neurologic impairment, anaemia, renal toxicity, chronic nephritis, reproductive impairments
Nitrous fumes	Bleaching of rayon (as stabilizer), textile industry, as intermediate product in many industries	Pulmonary oedema, bronchiolitis, bronchitis, pneumoconiosis, death

Organo-phosphorus compounds	Production and use of pesticides, agriculture	Severe poisoning, neurologic impairment, pneumoconiosis, pulmonary oedema, paralysis, death
Phosphorous and its toxic compounds	Processing of phosphates, fumigation of grain, mining, and the production or use of chemicals, detergents, explosives, fertilizers, fireworks, ignition compounds, matches, rodenticides, phosphorous bronze, rust-proofing of metals	Pneumoconiosis, pulmonary oedema, inflammation of the jawbone, neurologic impairments, damage to the central nervous system, anaemia, bronchitis, fluorosis, bone damage
Mercury (organic and inorganic compounds)	Production or use of agricultural and industrial poisons (pesticides), anti-fouling paint, acetaldehyde and acetylene, artificial silk, chlorine, electrical apparatus, mercury vapour tubes, rectifier batteries, silver ores, textiles, treatment of gold, mirror manufacture, smelting, mining	Neurological impairment, gingivostomatitis, psychosis, nephrosis, blindness, dermatitis, conjunctivitis
Benzene (and its homologues including nitro and amino-toxic derivatives)	Production or use of fuel, organic chemicals, reagents, solvents, additives in motor fuel, detergents, glue, paint removers, pesticides, phenol, shoe manufacture, styrene, plastics, resins, explosives, dyes, antioxidants, pigments, textiles	Central nervous system depression, anaemia, irreversible injury to the bone marrow, leukemia, dermatitis, cancer
Chromium (and its toxic compounds)	Production or use of chromium salts, chromium plating, leather tanning, metallurgy, refractory bricks	Asthmatic bronchitis, impaired lung function, lung cancer, ulceration and perforation of nasal septum

Hazardous agents	Sources of exposure	Health impairments
Arsenic (and its toxic compounds)	Production or use of fungicides, glass manufacture, metallurgy, pigments, preservation of wood, hides, fur or animal skins, smelting of copper ores	Conjunctivitis, visual disturbances, ulceration and perforation of nasal septum, neurologic damage, gangrene, skin cancer, pneumoconiosis and lung cancer, dermatitis, cancer of the larynx, lymphatic system or abdominal organs, blindness
Vinyl chloride, chloromethane and other halogen derivatives of hydrocarbons	Production and use of solvents, refrigerants, fumigants, plastic intermediates	Lung irritation, pneumoconiosis, neurological damage, paralysis, death (acute, severe exposure), cancer
Carbon disulphide	Industrial solvents, alkalis, cellulose, fats, oils, resins and waxes, manufacture of artificial silk by viscose process, pesticides	Neurologic impairment, reproductive impairments
Cadmium	Alloys for motor cars, aircraft, and marine engines, cadmium-nickel battery manufacture, electroplating, nickel plating, solder for aluminum, engraving process, yellow, red, orange paints used in ceramics, glass, leather, plastic, printing, inks, rubbers, vitreous enamel, fertilizers, pesticides	Pneumonitis, renal toxicity, cancer of respiratory tract and prostate, emphysema, anaemia, death
Nitroglycerine	Fabrication of explosives	Dermatitis, disorders of the central nervous system, hallucinations, cardiac impairment, death
Methyl alcohol (methanol)	Cement, coated fabrics, dewaxing preparations, dyes, inks, formaldehyde, paints, plastics, textiles, soaps, adhesives, resins, shatterproof glass	Dermatitis, blindness, irritation of mucous membranes, colic, insomnia

Carbon monoxide	Blast furnaces, boilers, garages, metallurgy, mines, industrial gases	Neurologic impairment, angina pectoris, death, reduction of haemoglobin in blood, lack of blood supply to brain, respiratory system diseases, pneumoconiosis
Manganese (potassium permanganate and other manganese compounds)	Ceramics, dyeing and bleaching of textiles, electrode coating of welding rods, glass, ink, paint, pesticides, fertilizers, steel and alloy steels, aluminium alloys, copper alloys, dry cell batteries, tanning of leather	Neurologic impairments
Respiratory system diseases (pneumoconiosis):		
Silica dust (chronic inhalation)	Sand blasting; cutting of quartzite; agate, gneiss, granite and slate manufacture; handling and transport of cement; mines and quarries; manufacture of glass, porcelain, pottery, slate; pencil, knife and scissors sharpening with grinding stone	Silicosis and silica-tuberculosis (pulmonary fibrosis), lung cancer
Coal dust (associated with silica), coal tar derivatives	Coal mines	Anthraco-silicosis (pulmonary fibrosis), lung cancer
Asbestos dust	Brake linings, cement filler for plastics, fire smothering blankets, mining of asbestos, safety garments, thermal and electrical insulation	Asbestosis (pulmonary fibrosis), lung cancer

Psychosocial hazards

Child labour damages children's physical and mental health; because of their premature incorporation into the workforce, they often have to perform tasks which are not suited to their physical and mental abilities and needs. Working children are more vulnerable than adult workers not only for physiological reasons, but also because of a combination of psychological and social reasons. Some children at work are under psychological stress. The motivation for them to start working and to retain the job is to contribute to the financial support of the family, which is a heavy responsibility at an early age. Children react differently from adults when exposed to similar risks. For example, child workers may prefer to face a challenge rather than be considered weak by the other playmates and therefore may attempt the riskiest tasks.

Regular employment or work deprives children of the time and opportunity to go through normal development at the most critical stage of life due to pressure for survival. Children who are exhausted, hungry or anxious because of work would be at a disadvantage at school as compared with their non-working counterparts. In most countries of the world today, where children are working, they do it for more hours per week than are legal for adults in those countries. Girls are especially at risk. Almost everywhere girls work longer hours than boys, often engaged in both economic and household activities, whereas boys are usually only engaged in economic activities. Due to the greater burden placed on girls, they generally have a lower rate of school attendance and completion. Work may also have a long-term negative impact on social development, when it leads to no education or poor education and low employment prospects. These children will always remain in the group of low-wage earners. In macroeconomic terms, work injurious to the development of children perpetuates poverty, by degrading the human resources necessary for economic and social development.

NOTES

[1] World Bank, 1991 and 1993.

[2] ILO, 1988 and 1991a. See also ILO, 1996b.

[3] ILO, 1995.

[4] Ashagrie, 1993; ILO, 1996a and b.

[5] Ashagrie, 1993; ILO, 1996a and b.

[6] For an extensive discussion see Richter and Jacobs, 1991; National Committee for Injury Prevention and Control, 1989.

[7] Satyanarayana et al., 1979.

[8] WHO, 1987a and b; Pill et al. (eds.), 1981.

[9] Ashagrie, 1993; ILO, 1996a and b.

[10] For an extensive discussion of the effects of work on the health status of working children see Annex I.

[11] Mancian and Romer (eds.), 1991.

[12] Berger et al., 1991.

[13] For a very interesting discussion on new findings concerning exposure of working children to toxic substances see McGuigan, 1994; Reed and Besunder, 1989.

[14] Weisburger et al., 1966.

II: Strategies to address child labour from a health perspective

1. Introduction

There is worldwide recognition that there is still a great need for further epidemiological studies on the health aspects of child labour, for example, on the toxicological, metabolic and pulmonary effects of exposures specifically on children. However, there is already enough knowledge about the health hazards associated with child labour to compel us to take action while these studies are being carried out. The working children of the world should not have to wait for another decade while we study the problem. Many researchers and practitioners consider that most of the negative effects of child labour come from specific working conditions which endanger the safety, health and development of the children involved. There is a growing conviction that national and international efforts should focus on the abusive and hazardous forms of child labour, giving them priority.

The following discussion intends to provide guidance for the development of a strategy to combat child labour from a health perspective at the country level. The model is mainly based on recent ILO research and technical cooperation activities. It should be kept in mind that much of this research is exploratory and often based on case-studies. Therefore the following approach needs to be field-tested in order to be validated and improved. The annexes provide a more in-depth discussion of the impact of work on the health status of children, including the possible effects of certain hazardous agents, such as chemicals. They include also a discussion on epidemiological methods which can be adapted for occupational health surveillance purposes.

2. A policy framework at national level

In order to face the challenge of combating child labour it is necessary to have a systematic approach and a basic framework to build upon. ILO experience shows that no single action can have a significant impact unless it is developed in the context of a national policy. The national policy should emphasize an effort to promote the welfare and sound development of children. The definition and implementation of such a policy/plan would be the primary responsibility of governments. However, other social actors such as organizations working for the defence of human rights, employers' and workers' organizations, the parents and the community, as well as other members of society have an important role to play. To be effective, such a policy should go beyond the mere statement of goals, and establish specific measures to combat child labour, along with the commitment of necessary resources and a clear division of responsibilities between the various social actors concerned.

Priority should be given to the protection of the weakest and more vulnerable. It should be recognized that it is the right of children to undergo a physical, mental and social process of development. This cannot be achieved without effort. However, whatever activity they undertake, it should be appropriate to their physical and psychosocial development and the efforts requested from children should be adapted to their strengths and weaknesses, giving them the possibility to develop and serve society.

In order to achieve better results, an overall **health strategy** to combat child labour should include a combination of *actions* that can be taken based upon our current knowledge and *studies* that should be undertaken to close the gaps in our current knowledge. The driving force for this strategy is to prevent child labour and to protect working children by providing them access to health care with a view to the progressive elimination of child labour.

The overall **strategy** should encompass both action that prevents child labour and interim measures to protect and rehabilitate children who are working. Such a strategy should establish priorities at national level and be reviewed periodically in the light of changing circumstances and the lessons learned.

For the implementation of the **strategy**, it is essential to define an overall *approach*, to establish *criteria*, to define *priorities* and *target groups* of working children according to local conditions. On the basis of these criteria, guidelines on the implementation of occupational health action at the national level can be developed. At the beginning, the criteria will be based on a number of assumptions on the grounds of actual knowledge. In the course of action, these criteria will become more precise and the guidelines will be improved through a continuous process of development of a conceptual framework, adapted in the light of experience and knowledge gained by practical activities and applied research at the national and regional level.

3. Priorities for action

As the issue of child labour cannot be resolved overnight, the top priority should be to prevent and eliminate the participation of children in those economic activities which are most detrimental to them, such as those conducted under slavery and those involving particularly hazardous or abusive conditions. Because children working in highly exploitative conditions are hard to reach, organizations assisting working children often focus on more accessible groups, such as street children, yielding quick results. The **strategy** should aim at seeking to reverse this trend, by ensuring that organizations receive the assistance required to enable them to reach those child workers most at risk. The initial experience of the ILO International Programme for the Elimination of Child Labour (IPEC) suggests that it is easier and more advantageous to prevent child labour than to "cure" it.

Top priority should be given to preventing and eliminating the participation of children in hazardous work and particularly abusive conditions, such as slavery or bonded labour. For the establishment of *priorities* at the national level, the following target groups should be identified:

— children in occupations known to be hazardous;

— young and vulnerable children; and

— victims of child exploitation and abuse.

The identification of children engaged in occupations, working conditions and working activities known as hazardous should be done at all levels, and in particular at the local level, because the danger of an occupation depends, to a large extent, on local conditions. Participating in home-based agriculture helping the family is a completely different situations from working during harvesting, on a piece-rate basis, as a member of the family of a migrant worker in a foreign country. Therefore, "most hazardous occupations" should be identified in the light of local conditions, common sense, current knowledge and experience, and on medical grounds, taking into consideration the perception of the problems by the local authorities and the community.

A basic distinction is whether the child works in the "organized sector" or in the "informal sector". It is less evident to find children working in the organized sector as, in most cases, it will be illegal. In the case of the informal sector, exploitation and child abuse are more widespread, have different levels and can lead to extreme situations such as exposing children to criminality and prostitution, where children are completely unprotected. The main objective is to promote some type of organization placing the emphasis on community participation and the involvement of the children themselves.

The elimination of child labour should be seen as a process which should be undertaken at the national level, i.e. a progressive elimination of child labour through an improvement in education, combating poverty and increasing standards of living; and also at the individual level where a child should move progressively towards rehabilitation and be given the opportunity to live in a safe and healthy environment, to ensure the provision of food and shelter and other basic needs, and to develop in society. Innovative approaches are necessary for the provision of health care and for health promotion in the community, both in the household and in the workplace. In many cases, this is the same for poor families engaged in the informal sector.

Occupational health has proved to be an effective entry point to improve working conditions in the informal sector. It could be used to develop programmes on occupational safety and health for the adult workers, targeting health promotion and awareness, raising activities for their children through a number of interventions.

The overall approach should be oriented to the following main purposes:

— to assess;

— to inform and denounce (create awareness);

— to provide health services;

— to promote health and safety; and

— to evaluate results.

4. Evaluation of children's working conditions

Although it is acknowledged that there is a lack of specific information on the health impairments of working children caused by occupational hazards, much useful information does exist in the areas of occupational medicine, paediatrics, and injury prevention which, if brought together, would permit an assessment of the health risks, addressing the most hazardous exposures and occupations. A systematic examination of the main hazards faced by children employed in specific occupations could lead to the development of preventive and protective measures.

Identification and use of sources of information

In order to have a global estimate of the number and proportion of economically active children worldwide, it would be necessary to have access to fairly reliable and comparable statistics from every country. At the moment, the available statistics on child labour provide a very partial view of the situation. It is virtually impossible to quantify the extent to which the figures are underestimated. The lack of reliable and comparable statistical data on child labour at the national level also make it impossible to study the trend of child labour over time and determine if it is increasing or declining.[1]

One of the difficulties lies in the collection of statistical data on child labour itself. Some countries tend to report only the adult economically active population. The meaning of "economically active" also varies according to the country. The population at risk is relatively inaccessible, concentrated mainly in the informal sector and in many different types of occupations within it. There is no record of those children working in the informal sector or of those working illegally. Available statistical information on child labour provides a very partial view of the situation since it only includes: (a) children with work as their principal activity, excluding those who combine work with their studies; or (b) those engaged as wage-earners, who account for only a small fraction of the total of child labour; and (c) children between the ages of 10 and 14, leaving out those under 10 years of age, which in certain countries may account for up to 20 per cent of the total.

In most countries, statistical information on children's injuries and health impairments is not linked to occupational data, and the distribution by age obstructs the identification of the relevant age groups. Most of the data available, (for example, compensation claims for injury) relate to adult workers. Data is lacking concerning the incidence and prevalence of injuries and disabilities of children and youth in most developing countries. Where information is available, there is little distinction between accidents of occupational origin and those due to non-occupational causes. To obtain this type of information, it is necessary to carry out special surveys or community studies.

As mentioned in the first part of this publication, there are some studies on the health, growth and development of infants, preschoolers and schoolchildren which demonstrate that severe and chronic malnutrition and severe growth retardation are related, resulting in a reduced pattern of gain in height and body mass as young adults. However, only a few studies have been carried out on working children and on the consequences of work on their health and nutritional status, as well as its implications on their growth and development in their adolescence and adult life.

Owing to lack of information, it is still premature to establish the epidemiological impact of different kinds of work on working children, particularly concerning growth and development, orthopaedic and musculo-skeletal disorders, poisoning, intoxication and premature death. Most of the studies dealing with the health aspects of working children provide general statements which, in many cases, are not documented by epidemiological studies or medical data, but based on the common sense of health professionals, i.e. what is dangerous to the health of adult workers will be even more dangerous for children who are undergoing growth and development.

In view of the inadequacy of existing information, special attention should be given to the conceptual and methodological aspects of the collection of data and elaboration of statistics on child labour.

The collection of accurate health data would permit those dealing with the health problems of child workers to conceive epidemiological studies and preventive programmes to improve the protection of working children. It would be necessary to develop standard methods for more accurate collection of data on the number of working children, on the number of children injured and made ill at work and on the circumstances surrounding these events. This information is necessary in order to:

(a) design interventions directed to protect working children. For this purpose it is necessary to know where working children are to be found and whether they are concentrated in any given sector, industry, occupation, or activity;

(b) appraise rates of injury and illness among working children to guide the direction of potential interventions. To this end it is important to have an idea of the age, sex and size of the population of working children at any given place and the type of hazard they are exposed to;

(c) obtain accurate information on type of injury in relation to type of work, type of equipment, working conditions, and part of the body injured (e.g. head, hand, leg, trunk) in order to propose preventive programmes;

(d) assess, using scientific evidence, the effects of hazardous work on the growth and development of children, denounce the health consequences and prevent them;

(e) estimate specific high-risk situations by field observation, for the development of measures to detect and prevent hazards; and

(f) evaluate the outcome of improved working conditions of children when specific hazards are eliminated from certain types of work, compared to when they are not.

Information on salary, method of payment (money or in-kind), hours of work, night work, school attendance and performance, work versus apprenticeship, reasons for working, family composition and socio-economic status would provide a better image of the socio-economic factors determining their working conditions.

From this data, preliminary calculations of work-related injury rates would be possible, permitting comparisons of these rates across age groups, countries, industries and occupations. This information would be useful for prioritizing an approach to exposures and occupations which require intervention, and to design practical intervention programmes on health protection for working children.

Taking into consideration worldwide existing available data on working populations which are relevant to the epidemiological analysis of the impact of work on children's health, the sources listed in Table 3 could be adapted or used in order to identify working children and evaluate their health status.

TABLE 3.   INFORMATION SOURCES FOR HEALTH DATA

National population census:
— Paid work by age group.
— Work-related disabilities.
— Socio-demographic characteristics of working children.

Surveys of population samples:
— National health or nutrition surveys: data on injuries, disabilities or specific health conditions.
— Labour force surveys: proportion of the child population receiving wages, number of hours worked and the industries employing children.

Ad hoc or special surveys (in-depth information on specific issues):
— Survey data on industries in the informal sector (Ministry of Labour).
— Child workers in rural areas (Ministry of Agriculture).
— Health and living conditions of child workers (Ministry of Health, departments of occupational medicine in institutes or universities).

Administrative records:
— Work-related deaths and other registries of vital statistics.
— Disability or compensation records (Ministry of Health and social security institutions).
— School enrolment and attendance (Ministry of Education).

Medical records:
— Disabilities or specific health conditions.
— Work-related injuries.
— Work-related diseases.

Limitations of existing data should be taken into account particularly concerning:

(a) censuses, because child labour is normally under-reported as it is illegal; some relevant data (e.g. number of years of employment) may not have been collected;

(b) ad hoc surveys, which may cover small and unrepresentative population samples;

(c) disability and compensation records, which are not usually available for the informal sector, where most children work;

(d) medical records, which rarely mention a child's occupational status or if a disease or injury was work-related; and

(e) school enrolment which does not reflect school attendance.

In order to gain sufficient knowledge on how many children are suffering the adverse effects of a particular type of work, there are basically two requirements which must be met: the adverse effects must be identified and such information should be collected and compiled in relevant registries. Central registries can be adapted to cover large numbers of children or large geographic areas to maintain data in the most usable form, accessible to health care providers, educators, researchers and legislators. Data need to be provided to those registries by institutions such as hospitals and clinics, but there is also a need for large-scale surveys of working children from the informal sector, to gather more data on the health risks faced by those children who may not have access to formal health care institutions.

Possibilities for central data registries of children injured/made ill at work include:

(a) those on a national level. Such registries could be maintained by the National Council on Occupational Safety and Health, the National Institute for Occupational Safety and Health, the Ministry of Health or other relevant national bodies;

(b) those at the state or provincial level. These could be maintained by the workers' compensation boards, by the Department of Health or by insurance companies which would be in a good position to collect data from all providers of medical care, including community health workers, physicians, emergency services, and hospitals;

(c) registries, which may also be maintained at a community level by a local health department or the medical records department of a local hospital. In small or isolated rural areas, records could be maintained by a community health worker. As far as possible, it would be ideal to use existing registries where feasible. For instance, poison centres could include a questionnaire in their database for all paediatric and adolescent poisonings to ascertain whether the child was poisoned in the course of work and, if so, what the circumstances were (e.g. Was the child sprayed by an aerial pesticide application? Did the accident occur when mixing powdered pesticide into liquid without any protective equipment?).

For both the assessment and the collection of the data it is necessary to provide specific training to those engaged in the task, in order to identify children injured or poisoned at work. Such people include community health workers, primary care providers, labour inspectors, ambulance and emergency medical care providers, police officers, fire departments, emergency service staff, trauma surgeons, family practitioners and paediatricians. They have a particularly important and valuable role in providing not only demographic information, but also specific information on the situation leading up to the injury. Inspectors and other persons who ask questions for accident investigation purposes need to be trained to ask the right questions and to understand their own important role in providing information that has consequences for the health, safety and well-being of working children.

Structures for the collection of this data for young and adult workers already exist in some countries, while in other countries existing structures would lend themselves easily to minor modifications allowing the collection of such data, as for example through a Sentinel Health Event. Examples of these types of structures can be found in Annex IV and Annex V.

The compilation and analysis of health data concerning child labour should also be approached from ethical grounds. It will certainly provide new knowledge on the health status of working children. However, communities should not be seen just as opportunities to improve health professionals' own knowledge and careers. There is equally a responsibility towards the communities that have provided scientists with such data; in return they should be informed about the risks they face, taking into consideration their cultural background their local conditions and their particular concerns. Their own remedial measures to the problems should be treated with respect, without assuming that "scientific knowledge" has all the answers.

Health status evaluation

The assessment of working conditions of children involved in hazardous occupations and the evaluation of the impact on their health are not simple tasks. A variety of specific hazards can be found in a single workplace. Some of them can be specific to the occupation (e.g. exposure to silica dust); others are determined by the general working conditions and can be found in most of the occupations where children are involved (e.g. physical strain, poor sanitary conditions, poor lighting, long hours of work, inadequate or non-existent personal protective equipment, exposure to noise, etc.).

It has to be taken into account that children within each occupation carry out certain specific tasks that may be different from those that an adult worker would perform. The tasks may also be different according to the age group (e.g. 12-year-old children will carry out different tasks from seven-year-old ones within the same enterprise). Therefore, children's exposure to hazardous agents and injuries in each occupation would differ from those of adult workers according to the types of task that they accomplish (e.g. the construction industry is one of those with a higher incidence of fatal accidents, and although children are not necessarily involved in the most dangerous tasks in this industry, they should not be involved at all). Similarly, certain working conditions that may not imply an evident risk for an adult worker could have serious consequences to children's growth and development on a long-term basis (e.g. carrying heavy loads or exposure to certain agents even in low concentrations).

A core list of health criteria to define hazardous occupations would be a good tool for assessment purposes. Nevertheless, the advantages and disadvantages of establishing a core list of the most hazardous occupations in hierarchical order, according to the information available, should be weighed carefully. It may give the false idea that child labour is not unhealthy and therefore is acceptable for certain occupations not covered by the list. It may also be very difficult to find sound and scientific criteria to decide which are the "most hazardous occupations". It is necessary to define:

— which health criteria can be used to decide which types of work are more damaging, taking into account the combination of physical, psychological and biological hazards, and the long-term consequences of hazardous exposure; and

— which criteria will be used to set priorities, taking into account specific cultural, sociological and economic realities in each country. In some cases, the criteria may be political and not necessarily health-related.

A first approach is to base the judgement on basic occupational safety and health and "common sense" using data available for adult workers (as explained already, such data will have its limitations). On this basis, we could identify the following sectors as being most hazardous:

— agriculture;
— mining;
— construction;
— manufacturing;
— warehousing and storage operations;
— transportation; and
— wholesale trades.

However, even with this approach the risks to children's health will depend on the types of task that they perform and, therefore, the hierarchical order may be different. It may be difficult to try to define broad categories of the most hazardous occupations, as the issue of determining which are the most hazardous occupations would depend on the task performed by the children and not necessarily on the sector or industry as a whole. In any case, it is evident that children should not be exposed to recognized hazards that cause or are likely to cause death or serious physical harm. In general terms, it can be defined which hazardous agents they should not be exposed to (e.g. organic solvents) and under which conditions they should not be working, based on information on the actual activities they carry out (e.g. dragging and carrying molten glass in the glass bangle industry).

For enforcement purposes, it would be more realistic to prepare a list of those tasks or activities where child labour should be banned as a matter of priority, instead of sectors or occupations. Table 4 contains an example of such a list:

TABLE 4.   PRIORITY LIST OF ACTIVITIES PROHIBITED TO CHILDREN

A *priority list* of tasks or activities prohibited to children, based on national legislation and ILO standards, could include, but not be limited to, the following:

— mining (including all types of work performed in any underground or open pit, or surface part of a mine or quarry, which contributes to the grading, cleaning or handling of coal or other minerals);

— excavation operations;

— manufacturing and storing explosives;

— handling or using blasting agents (e.g. dynamite, black powder, sensitized ammonium, nitrate, blasting caps and primer rods; anhydrous ammonia);

— wrecking, demolition and ship-breaking operations;

— manufacturing brick, tile and related products;

— roofing operations;

— operating or assisting with operation of a tractor or agricultural machinery;

— operating power-driven woodworking machines;

— operating power-driven circular saws, band saws, and guillotine shears;

— operating power-driven hoisting apparatus;

— operating power-driven metal-forming, punching and shearing machines;

— operating power-driven paper products machines;

— operating power-driven bakery machines;

— occupations involving the use of power-driven food slicers, grinders, choppers, cutters and bakery-type mixers;

— maintenance or repair of machines or equipment;

— motor vehicle driving;

— logging;

— loading and unloading goods to and from trucks, cars or conveyors;

— loading or unloading timber or other heavy loads;

— warehouse work (except office and clerical work);

— working in freezers and meat coolers and work preparing meat for sale ;

— slaughtering or meat packing and processing;

— work in or around boiler or engine rooms;

— outside window washing involving working from windows sills or requiring the use of ladders or scaffolds;

— cooking and baking (except at lunch counters, snack bars, or cafeteria serving counters);

— transport (by rail, highway, air or water, pipeline, etc.);

— working inside or in front of forage or grain storage and silos with toxic atmosphere or deficient in oxygen;

— working in a yard pen or stall occupied by animals which can be a source of risk (bulls, stud horses, pigs, newborn calves);

— employment resulting in exposure to radioactive substances;

— exposure to organic solvents and other hazardous chemicals used in industry;

— handling or applying agricultural chemicals and veterinary products, including cleaning-up or decontaminating equipment, disposal or return of empty containers or serving as a flagman for aircraft spray application.

A priority list is a good instrument of observation to guide action. However, in order to evaluate actual working conditions of child labourers in so far as they affect their physical and mental health, such a priority list has to be supported by other information, for example:

— an interview with the employer or person responsible for the undertaking (employer's present views and future plans for the children); and

— interviews with the children themselves (description of their working conditions and their own experience of ill health).

In any case, it would be necessary to carry out an *in situ* evaluation of the health status and the working conditions of children in the light of the local situations, as working conditions of children will also reflect specific cultural values and circumstances in each country that will differ from place to place, determining how hazardous the tasks performed are (see table 5). This approach would provide more accurate data on exposures and injuries, as well as on the main hazards for working children in each occupation. The information should be used to propose corrective and preventive measures.

For the purposes of the evaluation of children's working conditions, each one of the sectors, industries or occupations has to be considered separately and it will also be necessary to elaborate specific checklists for each worksite. At this stage, describing the main occupations in which children are involved (see Table 1) and hazardous agents to which they may be exposed (see Table 2) are a first tool for action.

TABLE 5.   DEFINITION OF TARGET GROUP(S)

A number of questions have to be taken into account when trying to define our *target group(s)*:

(a) *Child labourer characteristics*: They should include past and present occupational history. The determination or approximate estimation of age, sex, race, age of brothers or sisters, period of time in present job, previous work experience (type of activity and number of years), living with the family or not; living in the workplace or not; years of schooling and if he/she is attending school at the moment.

(b) *Family characteristics*: Whether parents are alive or not, parents' marital status, place of family residence, number of children, ages of children, how many family members work, income of the family, occupation and education of each parent.

(c) *The type of economic sector*: The industry, enterprise or occupation that will be considered in order to determine the specific indicators to be used, e.g. agriculture, construction, carpet weaving, restaurants, etc. If the workplace site is in an urban or rural area, this has also to be taken into account.

(d) It has to be decided if marginal economic activities, such as domestic work or street work, will also be considered.

(e) *Type of work arrangements* that could exist, e.g. seasonal, part time, full time; working for wages, non-wage children; apprenticeship, family-employed, self-employed; in each case special considerations are necessary.

(f) *Characteristics of the job performed* taking into account the age group, the division of tasks and establishing which of them would be relevant for their health and safety: general working environment and physical hazards (e.g. noise level, radiation exposure, temperature, illumination, ventilation, housing conditions), chemical and biological hazardous agents, working postures, occupational injuries, first-aid and medical facilities, social life at work and psychosocial hazards. Drinking-water facilities, availability of protective equipment and safety measures, availability of food at the workplace. Description of the tasks performed, duration of work (e.g. total hours of work per day, number of days of work per week, time of the day when work begins and ends each day, time travelling to work, holidays, resting periods during work), number of weeks, months or years at the present job, previous occupations, means of transport to work.

For further evaluation of the health conditions of the children, clinical examinations by a physician or trained health worker would be necessary, as well as biological sampling and laboratory testing (e.g. blood samples to determine anaemia through haemoglobin levels in blood; choline-esterase activity or chlorine levels in blood of children working in agriculture to determine exposure to organochlorine pesticides).

It is evident that for this purpose trained health personnel should be involved in the evaluation. This can be achieved through the introduction of a primary health care approach to the households and to the enterprises or workplaces, using community health workers. The health personnel should be trained to recognize the possible occupational origin of the signs and symptoms they observe, such as the detection of "occupational marks" (e.g. callosity of the hands, thickening of the skin, etc.). Children and their families may hide the fact that the child is working. Health personnel should also be trained in order to establish the relationship between health, work and diseases and for the recognition of specific impairments, disorders and diseases of occupational origin. A scoliosis may result from bad sitting habits at school for long hours, but may also be due to long hours spent in weaving carpets. Psychosocial and mental problems may result from abuse of solvents used as drugs or from an intoxication during work activities.

Table 6 gives some examples of the basic types of health data that may be necessary for the evaluation of the ill health of working children. For a more extensive discussion on the effects of work on the health status of working children, see Annex I.

TABLE 6.   HEALTH HISTORY FORM

— Age
— Sex
— Height
— Weight
— Immunizations (for major communicable diseases, e.g. tuberculosis, diphtheria, poliomyelitis, measles, tetanus, and whooping cough)
— Skin lesions
— Eye lesions
— Signs of chest problems
— Signs of deficiencies (nutritional, etc.)
— Visual acuity
— Audiometry
— Pulmonary function (vital capacity)
— Blood test (blood count, sedimentation rate)
— Haemoglobin test (anaemia)
— Urine analyses
— Other specific screening for occupational diseases
— Lead level in blood test
— Choline-esterase activity
— Organic chlorine test
— Any specific illness (endemic or infectious diseases) in the last month
— Mental health and psychosocial assessments

Recommendations concerning chemical exposure

According to developmental toxicologists, when health risks from chemicals are evaluated, the special characteristics of infants, young children and older children must be recognized. An appropriate methodology based on the knowledge of these differences should be used. Health care workers should be made aware of the special risks related to chemical exposure during infancy and childhood. Any work that involves exposure to known human carcinogens, neurotoxins, heavy metals, and substances which sensitize skin or lungs should be banned for children.

Asbestos is probably one of the best known of the human carcinogens. Children should not work in asbestos mining, construction, brake repair, or anywhere else asbestos is used, nor in jobs with exposure to silica or coal dust.

Aniline dyes are also known human carcinogens, and children should not be involved in the dyeing of wool for carpets or leather for shoes if aniline dyes are used.

Exposure to solvents and glues causes neurotoxicity and children should not be involved in work with these substances, of which perhaps the best example is the leather industry.

Many metals contain lead and mercury. Children would incur high mercury exposures in gold mining and should be removed immediately from this occupation. Lead is found in construction, glass works and automobile radiator repairs among others. Isocyanides and other sensitizers may be found in electronics work which should therefore be excluded for children.

While it might not be advisable for children to be involved in picking fruit or vegetables, children subject to the extreme conditions of sugar-cane harvesting should be a first priority for protection and removal. Children should neither be involved in chemical or pesticide formulation, nor in their mixing or application.

Preventive measures should take into account the special conditions of exposure to chemicals of infants, young children and adolescents. The establishment of an appropriate surveillance system should be considered. Clinical and epidemiological data should be collected following exposure of children to chemicals. Any increased incidence of a disease possibly related to chemical exposure should be reported and investigated. For this purpose, awareness among health care workers should be enhanced.

Developmental toxicology should be promoted and its methodology improved in order to include work-related exposure and better experimental studies. Studies to evaluate the risks associated with exposures during infancy and childhood to the toxic initiators and promoters of carcinogenesis should also be developed.

The development of a health strategy relating to chemicals should include the clinical and epidemiological data collection following the accidental exposure of children to chemicals. Toxicological follow-up studies should be made with children who have been accidentally exposed to chemicals that might affect the reproductive organs. These children should be followed prospectively to determine possible effects on puberty and reproductive capacity. If other organs or systems are likely to have been affected by chemical exposure, prospective studies should be made if possible to assess functional development, morbidity and mortality.

Exposure limits

Concerning exposure limits to hazardous substances, noise and heat in the working environment, it has to be taken into account that even if data on the effects of toxicological exposure on adult workers cannot be extrapolated to growing children, there is a special sensitivity to toxic substances which particularly affect the growing tissues and the organs which are especially active during growth. Occupational exposure limits do not apply to children. *Limit values for the public* should be used. For an extensive discussion on chemical exposure, see Annex III.

In the history of occupational medicine and labour protection, the approach was to prescribe lists of hazardous occupations where the employment of children and of young workers was prohibited, rather than to set specific exposure limits. This pragmatic approach was the only one which was efficient in the past, and probably it is still the one which remains valid. A first step would be to have uniform knowledge and experience regarding the tasks and occupations where the employment of children is prohibited in national legislation, throughout the world. *A fortiori*, it would be necessary to ban the engagement of children in work forbidden for young workers worldwide. In order to extend the list of hazardous occupations, a further step would be to review actual knowledge to identify those other tasks, activities or occupations which are obviously likely to be particularly dangerous. Tables 1,2 and 4 provide some information in this respect.[2]

Inherent in this approach is the need to create awareness and provide training to government officials, parents and children about why working in these industries and working with lead or other hazardous materials poses a health risk, so that they can make informed choices. Community, grass-roots level involvement is thus essential to ensuring that children are not banned from exposure in a certain occupation only to be exposed in another activity in even greater numbers.

5. An occupational health programme

There are a number of areas of action which can be addressed by an occupational safety and health (OSH) programme at the national level. The purpose should be to protect and promote child health by creating awareness about the negative impact of child labour and, in particular, about the damage that hazardous working conditions can have on working children's health; the impact that lack of education and training can have on their future development in society as adults; and the consequences to their well-being, dignity and personal achievement. In the implementation of such a programme, it should always be borne in mind that these are temporary measures with a view to the progressive elimination of child labour.

The main components of an OSH programme should include:

(a) withdrawal of the child worker from hazardous industries/ occupations/activities;

(b) technical and organizational changes in the workplace to improve working conditions in occupations which are not intrinsically hazardous;

(c) nutrition and health programmes at the workplace;

(d) organization of community support for the provision of health services;

(e) economic incentives to families; and

(f) training and education of older children in non-hazardous occupations through special programmes.

This can be done through a community approach which should be practical, participatory, action-oriented and should respond to actual needs. Such an approach should include:

(a) evaluation of working children's health status;

(b) the dissemination of information on health hazards and their effects, to denounce hazardous work and exploitative conditions;

(c) the protection of children's health and safety through preventive measures and access to health care at the community level;

(d) education, training and skill development through alternative educational methods;

(e) income-generation programmes to guarantee food and shelter for the child and the family;

(f) legislation enforcement and mobilization of the public and the community; and *most importantly*

(g) the active participation of children themselves in this process.

The training programme could include: literacy through non-formal education schemes (on basic reading, writing and arithmetic); guidance and instruction on safe drinking-water practices, sanitation, personal hygiene, basic occupational safety and health, food and nutrition, community development, budgetary aspects, protective laws and regulations, physical exercise and playing.

Some basic *criteria* to judge whether a course of action is appropriate or not are the following:

–   is income (food and shelter) ensured?

–   is there an appropriate degree of protection (health and safety)?

–   is there a process of education, a psychosocial development including the acquisition of skills and training?

–   is there community participation or involvement in the problem?

As regards community participation, the following *criteria* are applicable:

–   is the approach to community work practical?

–   does it respond to local needs?

–   is it action-oriented?

–   is it characterized by a high degree of participation of the children themselves, their parents, the community and the professionals involved in community work, including social life?

–   have strategies been developed to guarantee community surveillance and control of the improvements?

Action can be taken with the collaboration of:

–   community health workers, local NGOs, extension workers and other professionals involved full-time, part-time or on a voluntary basis in community work;

–   the parents, the traditional "chiefs" and the local authorities;

–   the children themselves.

Protected working conditions

As has been discussed above, there are hazards accompanying most types of occupations for children, but it has proved difficult to get them out of even the most hazardous working environments once they are employed there. Thus, anything that can be done to prevent the entry of very young children into the workforce would help to address this problem as a priority. It has been demonstrated on several occasions that parents, given a viable choice, prefer to keep their children out of the workplace and will utilize other available options. While this is clearly a social solution to a health problem, it is a strong mechanism for preventing ill health, and prevention is easier and more cost-effective than any other option.

When adolescents could be going through an apprenticeship process, various measures should be introduced to ensure that work is carried out under healthy and protected conditions. Information and training must be given in the workplace, mainly by the employer who has a definite responsibility, but also by older workmates and workers' representatives. Training is required on the development of skills, on the hazards they are exposed to and their prevention, as well as on their rights. This can be done initially at the vocational training school or during apprenticeship, and it must be effectively pursued at the workplace.

Improvements at the workplace can be introduced, including better working methods, safer premises and healthier working environments, as well as through the provision of appropriate tools, equipment and personal protective clothing. Due attention to simple hygiene can enhance safety and health. The careful management of working time, with rest periods and holidays and the elimination of overtime and night work should also be taken into account. In many cases, improvements at the workplace are relatively simple and inexpensive to implement.

It is important to consider preventing injuries, when it may not always be possible to prevent accidents that can cause them, by avoiding exposure and by using protective measures, protective equipment and adequate tools.

The early detection of occupational diseases is vital for the protection of all workers' health. Prevention is possible through the consistent application of adequate protective measures, effective environmental monitoring and control; adequate ventilation; the use of protective equipment; the provision of adequate information to workers who are exposed to hazardous substances, on adverse health effects and on the necessary safety precautions.

Extension of protection to other groups

Recognizing that there are areas of limited consideration due to the difficulties in its regulation in both developed and developing countries, there is a need to establish appropriate measures also to protect children working in family businesses and agriculture because available injury evidence indicates that they are also at risk, particularly those engaged in agriculture. Awareness of the family and the children about work-related hazards and other efforts within the community for preventive purposes should be encouraged and supported.

On rural plantations and in urban garment factories, many infants and young children are in the workplace because their parents have no access to reliable or affordable day care, and find it safer to bring their children with them rather than to leave them alone elsewhere. Children who come to work with parents soon begin to "help out", and at an early age they have joined the ranks of child workers. Therefore day care for preschool children is needed to remove them from the workplace. In some countries, crèches at the workplace or mobile nurseries supporting several workplaces have been developed as tailor-made solutions on a temporary basis.[3]

Access to health care through primary health care (PHC)

The primary health care approach can be used to reach working children in the informal sector. It requires a well-designed and managed primary health care system[4] that should be conceived within the framework of an overall national policy on child labour. Such a system should be oriented to poor urban and remote rural populations where most child labourers are concentrated. It should ensure substantial impact on the health of the "target population" in order to reach everyone or nearly everyone, through the adaptation of health care to local needs, even when resources are seriously constrained.

TABLE 7. PRIMARY HEALTH CARE PRINCIPLES

Primary health care involves:

(1) A commitment to the redistribution of health care facilities, so that "health for all" can be achieved. Inviting communities to define needs and priorities and seeking to respond to them. Community health programmes need to be flexible and able to adapt to changing needs.

(2) An emphasis on preventive measures as a priority, and on communities' health knowledge as a basis for prevention. The importance of preventive medicine is underlined in those developing countries where access to health services is limited, especially in rural areas.

(3) The demystification and democratization of medicine. Health care is seen as a common objective to which all can contribute and for which all community members are responsible.

(4) A holistic approach encompassing the whole health and development of an individual. Good health is not merely absence of disease, it is a state of physical, mental and psychological well-being. Health care in children involves care for their mental development and stimulation, just as much as for their physical growth and nutrition.

(5) A partnership between all with responsibility for health in communities. Modern medicine along with traditional ones. Development in agriculture, housing, sanitation alongside development of health services.

To combat effectively the causes of child mortality from endemic and work-related diseases through primary health care, health services should reach the community at the workplace and at the household levels which, in the case of the informal sector, are often the same.

Social participation and inter-sectoral action are necessary for the early detection of susceptible children and for the identification and control of risk factors in order to promote protection and prevention. The role of the health and other sectors is to facilitate the capacity for self-care and to promote a lifestyle characterized by health behaviours within the community, encouraging those elements which promote and protect health (health education, good nutrition, immunization, sanitation, availability of health services).

As the health of children at work is not usually covered by general health services, innovative mobile systems must be designed, especially for those in small and informal-sector enterprises. Many countries already have extensive programmes of primary health services which can be extended to protect a large number of children from occupational safety and health (OSH) risks. The strong link between the working and the living environments may well justify an integrated approach to the provision of general and occupational health services. For example, community health workers could have access to children at work, irrespective of the nature of the job and the form of employment. Perhaps the most efficient approach would be to work through public health staff, like community workers, nurses, physicians, health departments, to assist in educating others. Those in the health community who are already familiar with endemic diseases, occupational hazards and other work-related diseases can be trained to train others and to become sources of accurate information. It is necessary to act at a grass-roots level to provide health education to children and their families.

An adequate infrastructure of supportive services should be developed when providing occupational health through primary health care (PHC) to the community. The approach should be to provide universal coverage with health care according to the needs. We have to be aware that existing networks of health care facilities in developing countries do not always ensure effective services. The assignment of health personnel to provide health care to poor urban and rural populations does not always guarantee that these populations will be reached in an appropriate manner by those services. There are several limitations faced by developing countries concerning administrative aspects, planning, trained health personnel, financial resources, managerial aspects and wages.

For the design and management of occupational health through PHC strategies, careful attention should be paid to patterns of both endemic and work-related diseases, taking into consideration socio-economic and environmental factors which could determine the health status of working children. The PHC household-based services are designed to identify people at risk and to intervene before the disease strikes, through primary prevention (immunizable diseases), secondary prevention (catching a disease early in its course as in childhood malnutrition) or tertiary prevention (prevention of serious advance of a parasitic infection, as in the case of the management of diarrhoea). Children at risk can be identified at the workplace and in households, remedial steps can be taken and referral to secondary and tertiary health care facilities can be provided through the adequate training of community health workers on work-related disabilities. Community-based rehabilitation can use and fashion alternative methods for the health care of the disabled, by the construction of crutches, walkers or prostheses with simple, locally available material.

In the introduction of a joint programme on PHC and OSH, the PHC infrastructure should be built around community health workers (CHWs), local men and women recruited and trained in the community, assigned to workshops and households which they can visit on a weekly or monthly basis to identify the children working in the workshop, and visit them in the household, when possible. During their visits they should identify the priority endemic problems and the work-related diseases, and provide health information. Such initiatives could be part of income-generation programmes for the adult members of the family.

Within the training of PHC staff on occupational health, the concept of high risk at a simple basic level needs to be taught in order to recognize both general diseases and work-related ones. The CHWs should be able to utilize the risk approach, especially concerning the symptoms/signs/risks factors which might lead them to suspect the presence of a potential health problem requiring special care and referral, particularly concerning work-related conditions. Patients at a potential high risk will require more careful observation and follow-up arrangements for quick referral. A referral system in the community, or available to its needs, should be established to cover special diagnosis, treatment and health care. A prearranged system could be established for this purpose through the local health centre and the local and district hospitals available in the area. For this purpose, the CHWs should be supervised and trained by community health nurses and community health doctors who will take decisions about local health care or referral. They should work at the local health centre and have access to a front-line hospital.

Concerning the activities that the CHWs have to develop in the community, the training should include a combination of occupational health and primary health knowledge and other paediatric information for example and the assessment of malnutrition and children's growth and development.[5] The CHWs could carry out the following activities:

(a) act as focal points for local health personnel and for the collection of basic data on PHC and OSH;

(b) report to the health personnel (community health nurse, community health doctor) in the local health centre who supervise and monitor their training;

(c) act as links with the existing health infrastructure, local health centre and local or district hospital;

(d) provide preventive and awareness services;

(e) provide first aid and simple curative treatment (including the provision of essential drugs in the case of minor illness, supervised by qualified health personnel);

(f) provide health education (including information on communicable diseases or epidemics and work-related diseases);

(g) promote food supply and proper nutrition, safe water supply and sanitation;

(h) provide immunization and prevention and control of endemic diseases;

(i) promote appropriate prevention and control of work-related diseases;

(j) provide appropriate referral and treatment of diseases and injuries;

(k) provide information and referral on dental health and mental health; and

(l) administer aseptic techniques in child delivery.

Impact assessment

Because the data collection systems in developing countries are often inadequate, a comprehensive assessment of the impact of primary health care programmes and occupational safety and health programmes has not yet been possible.

In order to evaluate the impact of the activities undertaken in an occupational safety and health programme (even in a small project), a health information system can be built-up on information collected by the CHWs. The information obtained could be used for the management of health care of individual children and for community surveillance, through a Sentinel Health Event, for example.[6]

Community-based surveillance can also be undertaken through cross-sectoral surveys and through the Sentinel Health Events on a quarterly, semi-annual or annual basis, to monitor the impact of health programmes.

This information could be used as a basis for PHC management decisions, through a few indicators, e.g. immunization coverage, nutritional status, mortality rates of children from a certain age group (under 5 for PHC, from 6 to 11 for child labour, between 12 and 16 for adolescent labour). In some cases, the community shares the cost of the services on a fee-for-service basis, on a prepaid basis, or through contributions, such as land, cash crops or volunteer services.

Evaluation of the results of such a programme as in any PHC practice will be necessary, particularly in the case where available data for preventive purposes are limited. Therefore, the development of basic indicators (access to health care, access to safe drinking water, level of immunization, type of work, work-related exposure, temporal health problems, possible associations and a record-keeping system) is essential. Innovative approaches, such as mother's health records, and special surveillance tools such as personal health history forms adapted to working children, should be developed at the local level according to needs and practical conditions. For example, a disease condition may reveal paediatric implications such as a certain malnutrition level, which, when associated with chronic exposure, requires special attention, including inquiries on other children also exposed, identification of adverse health effects, diagnosis of toxic causes and referral to the closest poison control centre.

Some guidelines for influencing new health behaviours can be obtained from the Health Belief Model,[7] a home-based model which was developed during the 1980s as a useful tool for intervention in maternal and child care. It indicates risk factors and helps early intervention on PHC aspects. The World Health Organization has prepared a prototype of Home-Based Maternal Records (HBMR)[8] which was field-tested in 14 countries during the 1980s. In India, this model has been field-tested by traditional birth assistants (TBAs).

Some of the traditional methods used for the assessment of health status in children through PHC that were taught to the mothers are:

–   use of growth charts;

–   measurements for diagnosis of malnutrition (mid-arm circumference);

–   use of oral rehydration therapy (ORT); and

–   prevention and treatment of acute respiratory diseases.

The model could be easily adapted to include methods for the assessment of health status in children taking into account occupational health aspects.

According to this model, the parent (usually the mother) analyses a number of risk and barrier factors of child health and each new preventive behaviour, such as, for example, the benefits of providing immunization for the child. In this evaluation she will consider the degree of the risk involved in contracting a disease for the child, and the degree of the child's susceptibility to that illness. She will also evaluate the relative advantages of the social support and community reinforcement she will have if taking action.

As mothers traditionally play the role of health care providers, they are the best partners in this effort. They could support the programme through observation of the health condition of the child and record-keeping. Previous experiences of training mothers on basic PHC aspects such as hygiene, feeding, family planning, how to follow the children's growth and development, and recognizing the early signs of illnesses; nutrition; population sanitation; environmental sanitation; breast-feeding; childhood survival; immunization; management of diarrhoea; safe motherhood) could be improved further by including identification of work-related conditions and withdrawal of children from hazardous work, as well as improvement of working conditions and referral to appropriate services. In this context, involvement of women's organizations should be foreseen.

Involvement of the paediatric community

Paediatricians' input on issues of children's health and development can contribute towards identifying health hazards faced by working children. Paediatricians and child health personnel working in areas with a high incidence of child labour should possess at least a rudimentary level of knowledge on occupational medicine and the health hazards associated with various occupations where children are known to work. They would not necessarily need to be experts, but they do need to have sufficient knowledge to recognize a possible link between work-related illness or injury and the occupation of a child. Paediatricians could give anticipatory guidance to parents and young children concerning the hazards of child labour, consequently helping to prevent or delay the entrance of children into the workforce, especially if they are familiar with alternatives available in the community. They could refer to occupational medicine colleagues in order to include working children in their practices. This knowledge could be enhanced by the creation of multidisciplinary teams or local task forces of professionals in the fields of health, education and social services interested in child labour.

Rehabilitation

Rehabilitation activities and prevention of residual damage *(sequelae)* to the physical and psychosocial health of child workers should be foreseen in child labour programmes. This needs urgent attention in order to minimize the great functional and psychosocial obstacles to normal growth and development and to the performance of disabled children and adolescents as future adults.[9]

Major types of disability found in children in developing countries may vary from country to country according to local conditions. In the case of working children, some of the impairments are of endemic or congenital origin aggravated by work-related factors, in other cases they are a result of untreated work-related injuries. Some of the most frequent include: post-poliomyelitis, post-trauma fractures, burns, tuberculosis of bones and joints, cerebral palsy, mental retardation, epilepsy, hearing or vision impairment (due to vitamin A deficiency or to ophthalmia neonatorum), cretinism (due to iodine deficiency) and congenital malformations.[10]

In many developing countries, treatment facilities for disabled children are minimal or non-existent. Therefore, injuries are liable to lead to more severe and permanent disabilities as they tend to remain untreated. When children are victims of injuries, any resulting uncorrected disabilities are invariably longer lasting than in adults. The disabled adolescent has special needs because of the increase of self-consciousness and the strong need for peer approval during this phase of life.

Programmes and surgical correction of disabilities and rehabilitation programmes for handicaps resulting from injury should be developed on a priority basis. Aids for disabled children should be simple, reliable, inexpensive and the needs of the user should be considered in their design.

Children injured on the job must receive timely rehabilitation to ensure that they recover as much as possible and return to leading productive lives for themselves and society. Such rehabilitation should be made a social and governmental priority until there are no more children in the workforce. One possible approach is to use the existing infrastructure: providing the medical aspects of vocational rehabilitation through any such programmes which exist in the medical community, making sure that paediatric and school personnel are involved, and channelling payment through the same system that handles adult workers' compensation.

6.   Education and training

Information, education and training play an especially important part in the prevention of occupational hazards, and this point is stressed in many international instruments. For example, the Vocational Training Recommendation, 1962 (No. 117), provides that the training curriculum for young workers above 16 years of age should cover not only work skills and knowledge, but also health and safety factors involved in the occupation concerned. The importance of these problems can hardly be over-emphasized, as too often one finds that workers, and child workers in particular, are unaware of the exact nature of the substances that they handle, the risks involved and precautions required, either because the need to give this information has been overlooked, or because the information has been withheld in order to avoid alarming the users, an attitude which is both unjustifiable and dangerous.

In a number of industrialized countries with adequate legislation against child labour, many 14-year-olds are employed either in illegal workshops or in legal shops but working in illegal conditions. They are unaware of their legal rights and of the types of occupation prohibited to them because of their age. Their parents or guardians may be similarly unaware. Beginning to educate young workers about their rights and responsibilities in the workplace does not allow for sufficiently early awareness-education on child labour; information on relevant laws and health hazards needs to reach children earlier, before they start to work. For those children who go to school, one way to accomplish this is to develop and use modules which could fit into health education programmes.

In areas of the developing world where the immediate cessation of child labour is unlikely to take place, another useful model which has been successfully employed is to provide instructions in basic occupational safety and health to older children working in the fields, or in the workplace, providing them with alternative skills and non-formal education.

After-school programmes and other special programmes

The official system of education does not take into account the specific needs of these children. An alternative approach is necessary through the provision of remedial education, vocational training and skill development in community-based projects. Development of after-school programmes and day-care schools for small children, using the resources available in the community (e.g. households, workplaces, community centres, other public buildings), could be envisaged. Incentives for the selection of children attending this type of educational programme could be established with the selection of older brothers for apprenticeship programmes and employment, if the family agrees to involve young children in the educational scheme. One attitude which has demonstrated effectiveness is to support children in such a way as to empower them to know that they have a future, to believe in their own abilities and to have goals. However, it is necessary to do it carefully so that the goal is not just a child producer but a child as a future member of society.

Apprenticeship

Special care must be taken not to expose adolescent and young workers to risks or hazardous situations for which they are not prepared. It may be necessary to debar them from a number of jobs which would involve them in personal danger or in heavy responsibilities towards other workers, either because they lack the necessary training or are unfamiliar with such work, or because there is a risk of their being insufficiently aware of the responsibilities entailed or of losing control if a difficult situation occurs.

Although it is necessary to prohibit apprentices from engaging in dangerous work, as regards other activities, variations between individuals must also be taken into consideration. There are young workers of 15 to 18 years of age who work much more carefully, conscientiously and safely than many adult workers. One should also not forget that a young worker or an adolescent to whom one entrusts certain responsibilities usually makes a point of not betraying the confidence that has been placed in him or her.

The establishment of lists of tasks from which apprentices are debarred for their own protection must not prevent them from learning the indispensable skills and receiving the training required in order to perform such work in the future. In this respect, the Resolution of the European Economic Community, 1987, concerning limitations on the employment of children and young persons provides that action should be taken to encourage the timely initiation of young workers who may be called upon to perform work regarded as dangerous for children and young persons, when they have reached the minimum age for such employment. This initiation should be provided in the course of vocational training or apprenticeship and should in particular include instruction in the necessary occupational safety and health precautions.

Naturally, the other aspects of occupational safety and health, such as technical safety precautions, safety devices and equipment, organization and planning of work, choice of appropriate working methods and speeds, and safety campaigns, also play an important part in preventing occupational accidents to older children and young workers as well as to their seniors.

Access to education

Expansion of primary education is essential to ensure that, at least, very young children (under 12 years of age) do not work. Where schools are non-existent, distant or expensive, children are often lured into the labour market. The education and training provided should be relevant to the needs of those concerned. A number of studies report that parents are willing to renounce the children's economic contribution to the family, and even make an effort to provide their children with the essential material to allow them to attend school, when schools are made accessible and when they are convinced that the education is of reasonable quality and likely to result in higher earnings and in improved standards of living in the future. Therefore, innovative education and training programmes should be designed so as to be clearly related to job opportunities and future aspirations. Better access to educational and training programmes and the improvement of the quality of the curricula and of teaching methods would influence attendance rates and decrease the incidence of child labour.

Education, at least through primary levels, for all children should be universally available. It should be financially feasible for parents, in terms of books, instruction and uniforms, if applicable. Other programmes to make school economically feasible for the family could include the provision of jobs in the school to parents. A Dutch foundation has supported early childhood education programmes in developing countries in communities in which mothers are trained to be care-givers and educators, giving the mothers skills and income at the same time as providing care. Such programmes are an alternative to work for young children.

Efforts to train teachers should be supported, and this training should include basic knowledge in child development and health. The quality of education available may thus be enhanced and, in addition, teachers should be aware of the conditions of their students, so that the strengths of all children can be encouraged. For example, teachers must be educated about child labour, so that they are alert to the possibility that the child who sleeps in class or has erratic attendance may be working. They should know how to discuss this with children in a non-judgemental fashion, so that children struggling to survive academically are not belittled, but are given reasons to feel that school not only requires an important effort but is also a place where they feel comfortable.

Concerning adolescents, the experience of youth movements as well as ILO experience regarding special programmes for youth should be used. The ILO's Special Youth Schemes Recommendation (No.136), 1970, could, with some adaptation, be relevant to a strategy to eliminate child labour while permitting children and adolescents to survive and develop skills.

Health education

Health education needs to focus its attention on children through the inclusion of information on prevention of accidents and both endemic and work-related health impairments in the schools curricula through a child-to-child programme. This programme should be designed to teach schoolchildren to look after the health of their younger brothers and sisters and other young children from the community. Among the community, health education should promote dissemination of information about basic safety and hygiene in work practices, and prevention of accidents in the household and at the workplace, including practical information about what could be done to change the environment to make it safer.

Child-to-child method for health education[11]

The child-to-child education programme derives directly from the primary health care approach which has become so popular since the 1970s. It was conceived as an innovative approach to health education in primary schools and within the community, which involves children in the provision of health care in school and at home. It identifies many ways in which they can help themselves, younger children, their families and the community, through individual and collective action, sharing this experience with their parents, brothers and sisters and peers. The purpose is to provide basic skills and understanding in order to improve their quality of life and that of their communities through a primary health care approach. Learning to live in harmony with their neighbours, preserving their environment and taking care of their own health helps them to meet basic needs and improves their living standards.

7. Ethical aspects

Pilot projects should be designed and implemented keeping in mind the right balance between in-depth studies of the health situation of children employed in hazardous occupations and the use of this information for both prevention and the provision of health services to them. Assessment is necessary in order to guide the action and to promote awareness; however, any "research" should be clearly based on ethical grounds. It has to be taken into account that:

(a) looking for facts is most valuable if it is within the framework of a process of improvement;

(b) available information should be used to take action rather than to carry out further study which would delay the action or distort the allocation of resources;

(c) studying local conditions must lead to remedial actions to solve the problems which were identified: provision of health services, improvement of working conditions, corrective measures in the workplace, etc.;

(d) an ethical approach is necessary concerning the child as an individual and children as a sector of the population; and

(e) the particular sensibility of children to occupational hazards should be approached with current knowledge and experience to take immediate action in certain conditions, since psychosocial factors and local conditions might be much more important than physiological or psychological differences between a child and a young worker; current knowledge should be used for extreme situations, without requiring a lengthy and costly confirmation. What is dangerous for adults is obviously dangerous for children.

It is important to be aware that, when studying the situation, it will be necessary to identify needs. These studies may even create new needs which must then be fulfilled on a long-term basis. Assessment and research should be linked to the provision of health services. If the conditions are to be assessed, this information should be used to improve the actual situation, to increase awareness and to denounce, where necessary. At the very least, an appropriate balance should be established between the resources devoted to studying problems and the resources devoted to solving them.

8. Mobilization and public awareness

The need to inform, create or increase awareness and to denounce would vary according to the means of action and to the different audience to be targeted:

–   the children themselves

–   the children in school

–   the parents

–   the public

–   mass media

–   community health workers

–   governments

–   NGOs

–   women's organizations

–   community organizations

–   rural workers' organizations

–   national health systems (primary health care services, occupational health services, health education services).

The role of the social partners

While the main responsibility for protecting children from dangerous work and eventually eliminating child labour lies with governments, collaborative efforts by employers, workers and their organizations and by non-governmental organizations are essential. Employers, in their own long-term interest, should recognize that child labour is unacceptable and take specific steps towards its abolition.

Employers' organizations can encourage progressive labour practices by making employers sensitive to the special needs of children by protecting them, starting with the removal of the youngest and most vulnerable from the workplace. Other practices could follow, such as: training employers in first aid; promoting among them the provision of health and welfare services for children; informing them about child labour laws; and creating awareness of the fact that abiding by them is a way to protect their own interests and also save time and money. Workers' organizations should be more involved in child labour issues. They could play a key role in documenting child labour abuse, monitoring the enforcement of child labour laws; educating working children about their rights; organizing domestic servants and homeworkers and other workers under precarious employment in need of protection; and working closely with governmental and non-governmental organizations to reduce violations of child labour laws.

Non-governmental organizations play an essential role in protecting child workers by advocating effective laws and enforcement mechanisms, and by implementing programmes to assist and protect working children. They can act as advocacy groups by investigating child labour abuses in the workplace and collaborating with interested parties in pressing the appropriate agencies to take action.

Public awareness

The general public is not always sufficiently aware of the dangerous effects of child labour, or they accept them as unavoidable consequences of poverty. In many countries, people are not aware of the problems of child labour in general and of children working in dangerous conditions in particular. Making the most intolerable forms of child labour visible, showing their consequences, and indicating what can and should be done, are the first steps in the right direction to ensure that the most abusive forms of child labour become socially unacceptable and can thereby be eradicated.

Once public opinion has been aroused, it can play an important role. For many people, these conditions remain an abstraction, and actually seeing the conditions first-hand provides a powerful impetus for effective change. Awareness-raising campaigns can do much to exhibit child labour in hazardous situations, and to mobilize public opinion and political and community support. Because of the extent of the problem and the danger of apathy, efforts must be sustained so that the public and the relevant authorities are constantly reminded of these unacceptable situations, and of the need to take immediate and effective action.

Well-planned awareness-raising campaigns conducted through the media, at schools and in the workplace are an essential component of any national plan of action against child labour. The message should be simple and clear, refer to verified workplaces where children are employed in abusive conditions, and be adapted to specific target audiences. Dissemination can be done through radio (in local languages/dialects), television, films and videos. Comics and picture books widely disseminated among working children have proved to be effective in informing them of their rights and of the dangers of premature work.

Information on hazards to children's health and safety, through good statistical data on the number of working children and their injuries, would be a very useful and effective tool to mobilize public opinion on child labour issues. People need to understand the health consequences of child labour. When possible, it may also be quite appropriate to discuss the financial costs of children's health risks for employers, governments and society, to confront the argument that child labour is an unfortunate necessity. In those countries where child labour is considered as unavoidable, and is common among the very poor, economic arguments for the elimination of child labour have shown to be more powerful and convincing than emotional, ethical or moral ones.

Another effective way to mobilize public opinion into action is to take public officials and other key persons, such as journalists, along on unexpected inspections to places where children work. In rural areas, teachers can become effective agents in providing information to potential child workers, working children, their families and the communities as a whole.

In most developing countries, initiatives against child labour mainly come from non-governmental organizations. Many governments have restricted their role to enacting minimum age legislation but have been passive in its enforcement. Many trade unions have lacked the capacity to deal with the problem. Individual employers of children have always been reluctant to enter into discussion on the subject for fear that their economic interests would be directly affected by attempts to replace child workers with adults. Employers' organizations often face difficulties convincing them. Broader social mobilization is required, as the burden of the campaign against child labour is far too heavy for non-governmental organizations to carry alone.

Community involvement

It is necessary to be aware that when people live in conditions of severe underdevelopment (absolute poverty, no access to education, contaminated environment, social fragmentation, political instability, etc.), occupational health programmes through a primary health care (PHC) strategy may not be enough to provide health care to the community.

There are some obstacles to the implementation of PHC strategies reaching all the people from a given population. These involve social, cultural, political, economic and environmental factors. In order to achieve success, it is essential to involve the community, taking into consideration their interest, knowledge and participatory support, involving them in the decision-making process, and not only expecting them merely to cooperate in the implementation of decisions taken by health care providers.

PHC strategies need to be integrated with other development activities aimed at achieving a better quality of life. Effective inter-sectoral collaboration is necessary to support village-based self-managed development projects. Developing countries need first to review the existing local technologies, identify and assess their relevance and acceptability according to national and local needs, before importing advanced medical technologies from developed countries, which are sometimes inappropriate and expensive. There is also a lack of manpower to handle such technologies, the safe practices related to them and the maintenance of equipment. Appropriate technology should be developed and community resources should be fully utilized.

An important factor for the success of PHC is the use of appropriate technology. Appropriate technology means a technology that is scientifically sound and acceptable to those who apply it and to those for whom it is used. It should be kept within the local culture. Existing traditional practices and beliefs in health care during pregnancy, childbirth and child care in developing countries need to be reviewed and evaluated to make them readily available, acceptable, and of low cost. As child labour is rooted in the family's basic needs for survival, an effective programme on occupational health should take these elements into account.

Family members, especially mothers, can play a very important role in creating awareness in the household and in the community about the hazards that working children face. In realizing this, the community can help to decide if "the price to pay is too high". As crucial members of society, women could help in combating child labour through their involvement in awareness-raising, which would lead to self-reliance in the community and support for occupational health development programmes. In particularly underserved areas, women can participate through volunteer work, women's organizations, and parent and community organizations.

Strategies for communication and information dissemination

There is a worldwide consensus on the need for essential information on working children's health. This information can help save children's lives, and it can be used to alert parents and to create public awareness at a very low cost. However, information by itself does not lead to action. A period of time elapses between being exposed to a message and deciding to take action on it. Social psychologists have demonstrated that, in adopting a new health behaviour, a person goes through the following psychological stages: exposure to the message, attention, comprehension, belief, decision to act on the message, action and confirmation or rejection.[12]

There are different channels of communication that should be taken into consideration when we want "to pass the message through" concerning working children's health. This information needs to be supported by a broad range of changes in the community. Studies over the last two decades have shown that mass communication using multiple channels can be a very economical and effective way of exposing people to new ideas and practices and for creating awareness. This can be achieved through community organizations and mass mobilization efforts involving existing networks of influence at the local level.

In order to guarantee the effectiveness of the message, three factors have to be taken into account: the *medium*, the *agents* for change and the special characteristics of the *target audience*.

The mass media

Effective use of the media is required because reaching a larger sector of the population has a higher probability of success. With the growth of mass communication technology, radio transmission is present almost everywhere in developing countries. It can reach the farmers in the fields, the mothers in the houses and the small shops in the villages. The television network has also expanded very fast in the past few years; it has been estimated that 80 per cent of the villages in India and 85 per cent of the villages and marginal communities in Brazil can be reached through this medium.

The agents for change and interpersonal communication

Even more important than effective use of the media is a clear message. Comprehension depends on appropriate language, simplicity, illustrations and the use of analogies. An attractive "package" showing what to do and how to do it attracts attention to the children's health message.

For a large-scale health promotion campaign to succeed, interpersonal channels of communication should be combined with mass media to move most individuals to action. Potential sources of interpersonal communication are the primary-health-care workers and the community health workers who have been trained in many developing countries and who are in close contact with the communities they work with. Along with these are the voluntary organizations, women's organizations and youth movements, trade unions and cooperatives.

These people can act as agents for change concerning child labour. Among other factors, their effectiveness will depend on their technical competence, trustworthiness and their similarities in socio-economic status and cultural background to the members of the target audience.

When considering the target group, it is important to be aware that opinion leaders may be the community health workers or the more influential members of a community, women's groups or other social groups or church leaders. Opinion leaders within a social system are able to informally influence the attitudes and behaviour of the people from the community. Frequently, they may not have formal positions or "titles", but they may lead the promotion of new ideas or they may head an active opposition. Therefore, it is important to undertake communication activities with such people, persuading them to devote resources and time to the important task of spreading the message.

The target audience

It is necessary to be aware that the parents and other people within the target group hold values, attitudes and beliefs which may differ from the ones in our health messages. Individual change does not take place in an empty space, but rather in a continuous interaction with the surrounding social environment. Our message will fail unless we are familiar with the audience's present perception and behaviour concerning the health of working children, their attitudes, their beliefs and the social factors that determine such behaviour.

New beliefs and the decision to act are achieved through feelings of self-efficacy, knowledge about the resources and through the use of trusted sources of information, which are close to the target audience's own socio-economic and cultural background. Powerful influences on beliefs and decisions occur when the subjects identify themselves with the person transmitting the message and when they perceive a degree of similarity between the models and themselves.

Conventional media and extension programmes, intensive one-to-one contact and follow-up are necessary to reach those sectors of the population which are harder to reach. Those typically disadvantaged in their socio-economic status are more socially isolated and tend to be suspicious of organizations claiming to help them. It is among this group that the majority of child labourers are to be found. Even if such a strategy requires a long-term effort, it is this sector of the population which needs more child health-care services both from a primary health and an occupational health point of view.

Large-scale health promotion campaigns where mass media are appropriately combined with interpersonal communication efforts are necessary, but not sufficient to bring about desired changes in health behaviour. During the 1980s, child survival campaigns focusing on primary health care evolved from traditional extension and community organization efforts initiated by health workers to a broader social mobilization. In many developing countries a new social movement has been created with the active involvement and empowerment of local communities.[13] Unfortunately, little research has been done to analyse how individuals and communities acquire new health practices and change behaviours in response to these social mobilization efforts.

9.   Legislation and enforcement

The ultimate responsibility for protecting child workers and ensuring that national and international standards on child labour and children's welfare are observed lies with national governments. In particular, they should take immediate action to ensure that children are protected from dangerous work. Governments also play a key role in developing and implementing long-term policies to eliminate child labour. There are fundamental types of action against child labour which can only be provided by the central government:

(a) child labour legislation and appropriate enforcement mechanisms;

(b) national child labour policies that set public priorities and reach out to ensure engaging all the important social partners;

(c) publicly funded systems of basic education that ensure quality schooling that is physically and economically accessible to children of even the poorest families;

(d) effective policies and programmes on adult employment creation; and

(e) access to health care and social services.

Agencies responsible for these areas should develop coherent policies and programmes and coordinate activities so that limited resources can be brought to bear jointly on priorities with respect to child labour. Governments have a difficult task but, with commitment and political will, much can be done in spite of socio-economic constraints.

As mentioned before, most countries have adopted laws and regulations prohibiting children from working and restricting dangerous work by young persons. These national legal standards can be used as a framework for policy. Priority should therefore be given to legislation affording appropriate protection for children and setting age limits for different types of dangerous work, duly enforced by an effective system of registration, notification, monitoring and inspection. Accordingly, there should be provisions requiring employers to keep records of young persons employed and of the nature of the work.

The shortage of both labour and health inspectors, in comparison to the number of places they must visit, is evident throughout the world. Increased cooperation between occupational health and safety inspectors and labour standards officers could help in maximizing labour inspection. Shared information gathered from inspections would help to minimize problems of inadequate staff while increasing enforcement of relevant legislation. A trained and effective inspectorate is essential if the legislation is to be translated into practice.

A flexible approach would also be necessary in the context of labour law which requires the immediate dismissal or withdrawal from work of under-age children, as such action may in fact work against the children's immediate welfare. Action should be designed to provide both appropriate enforcement measures as well as facilities and specialized attention which are needed to provide a smooth transition for children from work to school and from school back to work at an appropriate time.

At the community level, change is enhanced and reinforced by national legislation and other regulations aimed at influencing behaviour concerning risk factors and their control. Additional requisites for the successful implementation of a national policy on child labour are efficient administration of health programmes for child workers, committed leadership and an innovative approach from policy-makers, programme planners, administrators, health workers and decision-makers.

10. Final remarks

Most of the negative effects of child labour come from specific working conditions which endanger the safety, health and development of the children involved. There is growing conviction that national and international efforts should focus on clearly abusive and hazardous forms of child labour, giving them priority.

The conditions under which these children work are common to most of the occupations: poor sanitation; inadequate workspace, installations and equipment; long hours of work; and low wages. Children involved in hazardous employment are exposed to toxic chemicals, hazardous physical and biological agents and ergonomic hazards. Under such conditions children suffer from fatigue, physical strain, aggravation of non-occupational diseases, and misdiagnosis of diseases attributed to non-occupational factors. They are premature victims of work-related diseases and incapacitation. In most cases these children are not reached by satisfactory health care services.

There is worldwide recognition that there is still a great need for further epidemiological studies on the health aspects of child labour, for example, on the specific toxicological, metabolic and pulmonary effects of hazardous exposures on children. However, acknowledging the lack of specific information on health impairments caused by occupational hazards, useful information in the areas of occupational medicine, paediatrics, and injury prevention, if brought together, would permit an assessment of the health risks linked to the most hazardous exposures and occupations. A systematic examination of the main hazards faced by children employed in specific occupations should lead to the development of preventive and corrective measures.

Even if the resources are limited, the protection of children from the most hazardous occupations, abuse and exploitation should not wait for structural changes or significant improvements in the general standards of living of the countries concerned. Independently of the country's level of development, a priority policy objective for member States should be the prohibition of child labour in hazardous activities and abusive conditions, for the protection of the youngest and most vulnerable. Besides the immediate measures, a national policy should include long-term measures against the underlying causes of child labour and attempt to control both the factors that generate the flow of children into the workplace and those that generate the demand for their work. In order to be effective it should be an integral part of an employment strategy that creates viable income opportunities for the poor through poverty alleviation programmes, alternative production technologies and strategies creating a more equitable distribution of income.

The child labour problem should not only be considered from a legal or economic perspective, but also in terms of the child as an individual with all his or her various needs. The approach should incorporate the needs of children for access to health care, suitable alternative education and vocational training facilities. In order to be effective, policies aimed at the protection of children at work and at the gradual elimination of child labour should be adapted to the socio-economic situation of each country.

NOTES

[1] Ashagrie, 1993; ILO, 1996a and b.

[2] For further information see also ILO, 1991a.

[3] Narang Spaak, 1990.

[4] According to the WHO's definition, primary health care (1978) indicates essential health care made universally accessible to individuals and families in the community by means acceptable to them, through their full participation and at a cost that the community and the country can afford. It forms an integral part both of the country's health system, of which it is the nucleus, and of the overall social and economic development of the community.

[5] For an interesting discussion on growth and development evaluation see Fescina et al., 1995.

[6] For a description of the implementation of a Sentinel Health Event see Annex V.

[7] Janz and Becker, 1984; Green and McAlister, 1984.

[8] WHO, 1985.

[9] WHO, 1989.

[10] Wallace, 1990.

[11] Hawes, 1988.

[12] Deeds and Gunatilake, 1989.

[13] UNICEF, 1989.

Annex I

The effects of work on the health status of working children

For the evaluation of the health status of working children, both public health and occupational health approaches have to be taken into account. A number of aspects of children's health have to be considered, including: children's growth and development, their nutritional status, endemic and work-related morbidity patterns, the psychosocial factors linked to their occupations, and their family relations. The following is a brief description of the main aspects to be considered.

Growth and development

Growth and development are sensitive indicators of a child's health. Outstanding evidence from several studies made since the 1960s has provided a better understanding of the overall process of growth and development and the importance of specific periods of this process, such as early childhood and adolescence. These studies have shown that all children, except for those from a few ethnic groups, have a basically similar growth potential.[1]

During the period of rapid growth following birth, the child is particularly sensitive to **environmental influences** and adverse conditions that may severely hamper growth. Both prenatal and post-natal growth vary considerably with socio-economic level.

Height and weight are the most reliable and simplest indicators of healthy growth and development. When the height-for-age of a child is less than the average height of a healthy population of children of the same age and sex, the child will be excessively short. When the weight-for-age is low, the child will be excessively thin. A child's weight-for-age can be low because of acute or chronic **undernutrition**.

The process of skeleton maturity is an important indicator of developmental age. Adult stature is determined by the speed of linear growth and by its duration until skeleton maturity. Taking **growth** as one of the best indicators of nutritional status, shortness of stature in child populations is probably due to the relation between nutritional status and infectious diseases rather than to genetic factors.

Impaired growth is a result of insufficient intake of nutrients to meet the needs of the body. With acute malnutrition (i.e. over a short period of time) growth in height may continue, but weight will be reduced. When malnutrition is chronic (i.e. over months or years), both height and weight will be affected. Only in those cases where malnutrition is severe and prolonged will bone growth be impaired. A chronically malnourished child who begins to receive adequate nutrition can regain weight, but may not achieve the expected height for his or her age after suffering deficiencies in height. According to some authors, smallness in size as a result of early malnutrition reduces physical working capacity in adult life.[2]

Morbidity

Those children who live in conditions of absolute poverty have higher morbidity and mortality rates, and reduced life expectancy. Poor health during childhood also affects later morbidity. In childhood growth, poor nutritional status and infections interact synergistically. The synergistic effects of malnutrition and infection are well documented. In well-nourished children both susceptibility to infection and severity of illness are significantly lower than in malnourished children. The impact of infection on growth is also lower and of shorter duration.

Infectious diseases and malnutrition are of major importance in developing countries. According to a large-scale study carried out by the Pan American Health Organization in 15 developing countries in the 1980s, nutritional deficiency was an associated cause in 60.9 per cent of the deaths from infectious diseases as compared with only 32.7 per cent of deaths from all other causes.[3] Morbidity data from these countries indicated that among the most common causes of hospitalization of young children are accidents, respiratory infections, infections of the gastro-intestinal tract, congenital anomalies affecting development, and neoplasms.

Endemic diseases

Disease and death are the result of multi-causal effects. The association of infection and malnutrition is frequently responsible for the initiation of the chain of events leading to severe morbidity and mortality in children. The main causes of ill health and death in children from developing countries are malnutrition, communicable diseases, diarrhoeal diseases and acute respiratory infections (ARI). Additional causes could be malaria, tuberculosis, parasitic infestations as well as other endemic diseases depending on local conditions. The overall infant and child mortality rate is due to a combination of these diseases. All of them can interact with one another synergistically and certain illnesses can render a child more vulnerable than others. During childhood and adolescence, psychosocial factors gain special importance in health and disease patterns. Interaction with socio-economic factors which determine the living conditions of children and their growth and development also have to be considered, in particular, in the case of those populations experiencing absolute poverty, having contaminated environments, lacking access to education and characterized by social fragmentation.

Diarrhoea

Diarrhoea is the most common illness among children in developing countries, and mortality caused by dehydration from diarrhoea is the largest single contributor to the mortality of young children. It is also a major cause of childhood malnutrition. Several studies have indicated that the highest incidence of diarrhoea is found among children between six months and three years of age, with the annual frequency ranging from 2 to 12 episodes per year.[4] Some authors consider that growth retardation is more closely linked to recurrent infections than to the availability of food. Although diarrhoea is known to have an adverse effect on growth through three independent mechanisms (reduced ingestion of food, metabolic changes and poor absorption of nutrients), few studies have estimated the magnitude of this effect. The results of one of these studies indicated that the prevalence of diarrhoea was influencing a retardation on the increase in weight and length, however, diarrhoea was more closely related to the reduction of weight. As other authors have suggested, this difference may be attributable to the fact that weight increases were measured over short intervals, and so the affected children did not have time to make up the weight deficit.

Vitamin A deficiency

During the first few months of life, breast milk is the primary source of vitamin A. An association between vitamin A deficiency and infections has been reported. According to studies in Indonesia, even a mild vitamin A deficiency predisposes children to an increased risk of diarrhoea and respiratory infections. Diarrhoea also lasts longer and is more severe in malnourished children. Worldwide estimates from the 1980s indicated that there were 700,000 new cases per year of insufficiency of vitamin A among preschool children. Of these some 60 per cent died and 25 per cent of the survivors remained totally blind *(xerophthalmia)*. This represented about 250,000 children becoming blind or partially blind each year. About three million children under 10 years of age became blind from this cause, of whom over a million are in India.[5]

Iron deficiency

Iron deficiency is the most common cause of nutritional anaemia in young children and women of reproductive age. Anaemia is mainly due to dietary deficiency of iron, poor absorption, intestinal parasites, and, in many countries, malaria.

Iodine deficiency

Iodine (thyroid hormone) is essential for the normal growth and development of the foetus, the infant and the child, and for the normal physical and mental activity of adults. Its deficiency provokes goitre (enlargement of the thyroid gland which causes swelling of the neck), reduced mental function, and increased rates of stillbirths and infant mortality. The effects of the deficiency are more serious during foetal life and in the first two years of life.

Acute respiratory infections (ARI)

Acute respiratory infections, measles, malaria and tetanus are other major causes of death in childhood in developing countries. In the case of acute respiratory infections (ARI) the incidence may not be affected by the nutritional status, but the seriousness and frequency of complications and death may be affected by the degrees of vulnerability of the child and the onset of the problem.

These infections are responsible for high morbidity of children all over the world in developing countries. Mortality due to ARI may reach 1,000 or more for 100,000 live births as compared to 30 per 100,000 in industrialized countries. Most infections are limited to the upper respiratory tract but about 5 per cent involve the lower respiratory tract.

ARI of the upper respiratory tract (URI) include the common cold, sinusitis, pharyngitis, tonsillitis and otitis media. Lower respiratory tract infections involve laryngo-tracheo-bronchitis and epiglottitis, acute bronchitis, bronchiolitis and pneumonia.

According to some authors air pollution is associated with an increased incidence of acute lower respiratory tract infections. Indoor air pollution from biomass fuels in rural areas (caused by wood, cattle dung and crop residue fires used for cooking) has been reported to be a contributing factor in ARI. Smoke and overcrowding may also predispose a child to respiratory illnesses.[6]

Malnutrition

Infant, child and adolescent mortality constitutes a strong indirect indicator of the quality of life as well as the psychosocial and physical potential of a community to survive. Malnutrition is the major health problem in the world today among working and non-working children, and is both an underlying and a contributing cause of child mortality in developing countries. According to the WHO and UNICEF, malnutrition is a contributing cause in approximately one-third of all child deaths. Furthermore, 14 million children under five die each year, most of them from potentially preventable causes. In the 1980s, it was estimated that in developing countries 12 per cent of children under the age of five suffer from acute malnutrition and that almost 40 per cent suffer from chronic malnutrition.[7] Malnutrition is often an important contributory factor, as 60 per cent of child deaths are in part due to the mortality of children made too frail by malnutrition to respond adequately to the worst effects of illness. More than half of the next generation is growing up undernourished.

The outstanding manifestations of undernutrition in children are:

(a) retardation of growth and development; and

(b) specific nutritional deficiency signs (protein-energy malnutrition, vitamin A deficiency, iron deficiency and iodine deficiency diseases are the most important).

Nutrition during infancy is crucial, because this is the critical period for the growth and development of the brain and other components of the central nervous system. This process begins during the last months of intra-uterine life and extends into the early postnatal years. The nutritional status of a child is influenced not only by diet and feeding practices but also by the frequency of infectious diseases. Repeated episodes of diarrhoea and infections reduce the child's resistance to further diseases, and increase the risk of a fatal outcome. Severely malnourished children have a 20 times greater risk of dying than their normal peers.

Synergistic effects of malnutrition on working and non-working children

A comparative longitudinal study between schoolchildren and working children was carried out over a period of 17 years in India to evaluate the effects of undernutrition during childhood on adult nutritional and general health status.[8] These working children were engaged in agriculture (as wage-earners or working with the family), in small-scale industries and as helpers in the service sector.

The study covered the entire growth period from infancy to adulthood and showed that working children suffered significant growth deficits as compared with schoolchildren. Even though at the beginning of the study there were no differences in the initial height and weight patterns, the growing pattern of working children was reduced, gaining lower height and weight as adults than schoolchildren. Most "normally nourished" boys attained adult height at a younger age and some of the severely undernourished boys were delayed in completing their growth in the overall sample. Working children grew up shorter and lighter and their body size as adults was affected as compared with non-working children. The results showed that severe malnutrition before the age of five impaired the capacity of linear growth in both populations.

In another study carried out at the beginning of the 1980s in South Africa[9] there was a high incidence and prevalence of retarded psychomotor development in childhood due to preventable causes associated with severe malnutrition (kwashiorkor or marasmus) in all cases.

In 1984, the World Health Organization carried out a series of comparative case studies on the effects of work on the growth and development of working and non-working children in some developing countries (Nigeria, India, Malaysia and the Republic of Korea).[10] In these studies it was found that working children had more musculo-skeletal disorders due to ergonomic hazards, poorer nutritional status, lower haemoglobin levels, higher incidence of respiratory and gastro-intestinal diseases, headaches, fatigue and vision problems. It was also found that, even though differences in weight were not significant, working children were shorter than those attending school. A lower rate of growth was explained by the authors as due to excessive energy expenditure, frequent illnesses, insufficient health care and psycho-social stress. The effects of early malnutrition on growth also influenced a reduction of physical work capacity.

However, it has to be highlighted that in most poor populations nutritional status, sanitation, daily environmental conditions and certain kinds of illnesses are present in both working and non-working children. Therefore, it is difficult to isolate a specific adverse effect of work which affects growth and development, using the available information.

Psychological and social development

The roles and functions of children in each society are determined by a combination of economic, social and political factors. The work of children may be participatory or exploitative. The health status of children will be affected differently if they are doing light work under protected family-based activities rather than working in hazardous or abusive conditions as child labourers. In some cases, children's work can be considered as a process of integration into adult life. In rural areas children start working between the ages of 5 and 15 years. In most developing countries, the participation of children from low-income families in different types of economic activity at an early age may be considered as an essential strategy for the generation of income for the family, the transmission of skills, the development of attitudes towards work and children's future integration into the labour market. In industrialized countries, the participation in the workforce of children below 15 years of age is not frequent. However, the performance of some type of light work during holidays or within the household is encouraged. Many people in both developing and industrialized countries feel that families should be able to count on children to assist in maintaining the household economy, and that such participation is considered desirable as long as it does not become abusive.

In mid-childhood (between the ages of 6 and 12 years) there is an improvement in visual and motor abilities and a longer attention span, which allow the child to learn reading and writing skills. There is also a considerable development of language skills, imagination and other intellectual abilities. During this period children also develop a social conscience and a sense of responsibility. School is very important at this age as it contributes to socialization and it introduces them to the culture of their society and to social rules and values. In order to learn, children need adequate memory, attention, motivation and freedom from fear and anxiety. Playing also has an important role in the process of interaction and development of self-confidence. It also leads to the acquisition of new physical and intellectual skills. It develops mutual respect as a consequence of cooperation among children.[11]

Children need the time and opportunity to experience childhood: to play and to explore, to develop family relationships and to learn from society. Restricted social interaction, long hours of work, heavy responsibilities and the lack of social support have far-reaching negative effects on their emotional and moral development.

Adolescent health

In most countries, the age of admission to employment is well above the age of puberty and consequently work during adolescence (i.e. 12 to 14 or 16) is included under the domain of child labour. The risk of physical damage due to work decreases with age; however, other health risks appear.

Adolescence is a period of transition between childhood and adulthood in which the body develops in size, strength and reproductive capacity. The mind becomes capable of more abstract thinking, further orientation and ethical conviction. Social relationships move to a wider horizon than family relations, where peers and other adults play more significant roles. Adolescents continue to need strong material and psychological support, and at the same time it is important to encourage them and give them the opportunity for independence, adventure and accomplishment. Adolescents can choose series of patterns which promote their own health and that of their society, or embark on lifestyles which are likely to provoke lasting harm to themselves and others.

The transition from childhood to adulthood itself sometimes leads to diminished self-esteem as the individual begins to question his or her own identity, sexuality, appearance and sense of self-efficacy. Failure is acutely felt at this time of life, especially in relation to new experiences, but the wish to be less dependent upon elders may reduce willingness to disclose difficulties. In stressful situations, the adolescent may be left with a sense of growing despair and hopelessness, and turn to suicide as a tragic solution.

Many of the health problems which arise during adolescence are direct consequences of behaviour, although there are many factors which contribute to such acts. The majority of deaths occur in healthy and potentially productive young people. Even though homicide and suicide are the major causes of death of young people, consumption of alcohol and pregnancy-related deaths are leading causes of accidental death.

Normal physical development during adolescence may be adversely affected by inadequate diet, excessive physical stress or pregnancy before physiological maturity is attained. In the absence of immunity, harm arising from infectious diseases (e.g. paralysis from poliomyelitis) tends to be more frequent and more severe. Children who have had serious respiratory diseases or undernutrition may fail to attain full adult growth and perhaps full psychosocial development.

Poor health during infancy and childhood due to impoverished working and living conditions can also have adverse effects on the health of adolescent workers. The impact of childhood diseases, toxic exposure or infections in infancy and childhood may become apparent only after years. Minimal brain damage, and visual and auditory or speech defects due to occupational exposure may cumulatively affect the adolescent's ability to learn and consequently his or her aspirations and self-esteem.

Every child should progress through childhood and adolescence with good physical and psychological health. The evolution of the processes of growth and development is the expression of the health level reached by children. Good nutrition, disease prevention and early diagnosis and treatment, adequate physical and social environments, fertility control, hygienic habits, early stimulation and establishment of effective bonds are conditions for normal growth and development.

NOTES

[1] Tanner et al., 1966; Tanner, 1961; Cusminsky et al., 1986; Fescina, 1993; Bennett, 1991.

[2] WHO, 1987c and 1988; Alleyne et al., 1977; Terra, 1988.

[3] Guerra de Macedo, 1988.

[4] Azevedo, 1993.

[5] United Nations, 1987; Puffer and Serrano, 1973.

[6] Kumar et al., 1990.

[7] WHO, 1987d.

[8] Satyanarayana et al., 1986.

[9] WHO, 1983. Child labour was widely practised and about half of the black population was under 15 years of age. The study included African, Mestizo and Indian children.

[10] WHO, 1987a and b.

[11] WHO, 1988.

Annex II

Examples of hazardous occupations and their consequences for the health of working children

In this section we attempt to discuss each of the major industries or sectors in which children are employed, what type of work children do in each of these industries, and the relevant hazards involved. The following list is not exhaustive, so there will surely be children employed in situations which are not mentioned here. The intention is to provide a practical summary which might be used as a reference in the evaluation of the working conditions of children and the possible consequences to their health. We have tried to provide basic information which could be of use to a broad audience, ranging from basic guidance for a labour inspector about the elements to consider in the risk assessment of a particular workplace where children work, to basic reference on possible occupational diseases for a physician examining a child worker as a patient.

Agriculture

Children can be found working in agriculture across all countries of the world. While many have traditionally been employed in family enterprises, children also work in large-scale commercial plantations and in agriculture as migrant farm workers, usually alongside their parents, often in situations of indirect employment where only the head of the family is actually employed, but where he or she is paid according to the amount of fruit or vegetables that are turned in at the end of the day. With more hands to help, the family makes more money. These children work long hours, sometimes over 60 hours a week. The most extensive literature concerning work-related injuries and intoxication of children is from agricultural occupations.[1]

Children are engaged in diverse agricultural tasks according to their age group. The main hazards which can be considered are: machinery, biological and chemical exposures, as well as dust-related and infectious diseases. Children are more likely to be killed by a tractor overturning, or by trucks and heavy wagons which are brought into the fields to transport the products, than to die from any other cause. In many countries children can be found loading hay on to high wagons, working around corn loaders, grain augers, power-take-offs and other large farm machinery. They usually work near to dangerous farm equipment or even operate it; they use a diversity of lawnmower blades from hand-pushed to gasoline-powered mowers. This can provoke serious injuries and even death if the moving parts of the machine are not equipped with safety guards. By the age of 12 many children on farms or plantations might be driving large tractors without supervision. In Australia and the United States almost 30 per cent of farm boys are driving tractors between the ages of seven and nine, and by then many more of them are already riding as passengers on tractors.

Children cut hay, cane and weeds by hand tools; herd and milk goats and cows and care for other farm animals; and carry and lift baskets and bags containing crops. Heavy lifting, carrying and prolonged stooping and bending affects the musculo-skeletal development of children.

Children can be found mixing, loading and applying pesticides, fertilizers or herbicides, some of which are highly toxic and potentially carcinogenic. Children in some countries from Asia and Latin America hold flags, to guide planes spraying pesticides as they fly over the fields, and this places them at a higher risk than adults. Usually they perform their tasks without any training or personal protective equipment and clothing, being directly exposed to poisoning through the skin and respiratory routes. Frequently there is lack of washing facilities in the farms and plantations, not allowing children and adults to wash off the residue of pesticides. Improper pesticide storage and disposal of empty containers and waste are also frequent, being the cause of intoxication and death when containers are used for other purposes or when children play with empty containers.

In the United States children of migrant and seasonal workers are working next to their parents. In 1990 there were four million migrant and seasonal workers with their children hired to work in labour-intensive worksites. According to a survey of 614 farmers from the Washington Association of Apple Growers, carried out in 1989, more than 98 per cent of them reported employing minors. Of around 2,500 children, 73 per cent were under 16 years old and almost 97 per cent of them were working with an older family member.[2] As most of the time they are paid on a "piece-rate" basis, migrant and seasonal workers need their children to work in order to survive. Another reason why parents bring their children to the fields is that there is a lack of day-care services for children in rural areas, therefore infants and young children are exposed to some of the same occupational hazards as their parents, even if they are not working. Children are also at a high risk of contracting parasitic and other infectious diseases due to poor sanitary conditions in the fields and in their housing facilities. Housing of plantation and migrant workers is characterized by inadequate and overcrowded installations, no heating, poor ventilation and insanitary conditions, deficient sanitary facilities and non-potable drinking water, which enhance the spread of communicable diseases such as upper respiratory tract infections, influenza and tuberculosis.

Because of the proximity of the houses of rural workers to the fields, exposure to residues of pesticides in the soil and foliage is common. In some countries it is a general and misguided practice to apply pesticides at the same time that work in the fields is undertaken, for example during harvesting, or to work in the fields still wet from spraying drift, exposing the workers to a significant and unnecessary risk. Pesticide exposure poses a considerably higher risk to children than to adults as the developmental organ systems are more vulnerable than those of adults with the same level of exposure. Some studies have linked pesticide exposure to an increased risk of cancer, neuropathy, neurobehavioural effects and immune system abnormalities. Such exposure can have other long-term adverse health effects.[3]

Whole population studies in Asian developing countries on pesticide poisoning have suggested that deaths from pesticide poisoning are higher than official estimates, exceeding 3 million cases a year.[4] An epilepsy epidemic in the Lakhumpur Kheri district of India has been attributed to the toxicity of the pesticide benzene hexachloride which is used as a grain preservative.[5]

Further research, especially for children, is necessary on the type of injuries, the risk and agents involved in each case and the necessary preventive measures.

Mines

Children working in small-scale mines can still be found in some countries in Africa, Latin America and Central Europe. Twenty per cent of child labour in mines is still done legally. The minimum age for working in mines in most countries is between 14 and 18 years old; however, in some countries permission to use children in mines starts at the age of seven years.

Children can be found working in quarries, opencast mines or in small underground mines, helping adult workers in some tasks. They might be working near their parents, as most mineworkers live together with their families near the mine site and, in most cases, the miners' income is not sufficient to support the family, so that the children also have to work. In small-scale mining, there are no limits on the length of daily working time or occupational safety and health regulations. In many cases, first-aid and medical facilities near the workplace are not available, and workers have no access to rehabilitation or social security schemes, no mandatory schooling or vocational training. Under these circumstances, children can be working for 12 hours a day with only 30- to 60-minute breaks, without provision of adequate protective equipment, clothing and training. They are exposed to high humidity levels, to extreme high or low temperatures; sometimes, if working inside the mine, they have to adopt awkward positions while working such as bending over, kneeling or lying down.

Hazards in this sector include physical strain, fatigue and musculo-skeletal disorders, as well as serious injuries from falling objects and tools. Exposure to harmful dusts, gases and fumes can cause respiratory diseases that can develop into silicosis, pulmonary fibrosis, asbestosis and emphysema after some years of exposure. Mercury poisoning is frequent in gold mining. Poor sanitary conditions are common, including no facilities to wash themselves after work or no access to potable drinking water. Some children engaged in bonded labour suffer from abuses and early death.

Construction

Child labour in construction is common in Africa, Asia and Latin America. In many cases, the worker and his (or her) family live on the construction site until the work is completed and everybody participates while small children play near their parents. Children, in comparison with adults, are involved in light work because work on construction sites requires certain strength or skills. Working children are engaged mainly in construction-related industries, such as brick manufacture including tiles, cement mixing, steel work in windows, furnishing, painting and electrification.

Hazards may include: electrocutions, falls from improperly built scaffolding and heights, cave-ins with un-reinforced trenches; extreme weather conditions and exposure to intense heat; risk of tetanus due to wounds from nails or other metallic objects; physical strain, musculo-skeletal disorders and fatigue, and serious injuries from carrying heavy loads; head, hand and foot injuries from falling objects and tools; health impairments from noise and vibration; injuries from being run over by heavy equipment; eye injuries from flying material; explosion and fire hazards and toxic fumes from burning substances; toxic chemicals exposure including tars, plastic foams (TDI), oils, adhesives, varnishes and organic solvents in painting, thinning and cleaning; chronic respiratory infections from exposure to hazardous fibres such as asbestos and fibreglass, and exposure to hazardous dusts such as silica, prefabricated concrete, lime and cement with additives, and dermatitis due to contact with clay or other substances.

Manufacturing (small workshops)

Textile workshops — The textile industry is one of the most widespread industries in the world. In Asia, children of 6 to 14 years of age frequently work in textile mills 12 to 14 hours a day, 7 days a week, often in unhealthy working conditions.[6] In this industry, children are exposed to a variety of accidents and diseases. The type of equipment used can vary from primitive hand looms used in textile mills (cottage industry) to more sophisticated machines such as those used in modern factories. Many of the old textile mills are powered by old machines, most of which are unguarded. The types of activities carried out include spinning, weaving, knitting and finishing natural and synthetic fibres.

Injuries and serious accidents such as loss of fingers or hands can occur when manipulating unguarded machinery. The most dangerous machines or parts of machines are those used in the opening and carding processes, like the gear wheels of spinning machines, flying shuttles, and the intake "nip" of finishing machines if they are old and not provided with guards, or when guards are not used. Musculo-skeletal disorders are frequent due to lifting and carrying heavy loads, particularly in woollen, jute, flax and carpet manufacture.

Large quantities of fibre dust accumulate on the ceiling joists, overhead pipes, window ledges and on the machines due to the process of weaving, flax breaking and spinning, including the periodic cleaning of the machines themselves. As housekeeping is poor in these workshops there is also an accumulation of cellulosic rubbish on the floor which is easily ingestible and respirable, provoking irritation of the respiratory tract from exposure to airborne dusts of cotton, flax, soft hemp and other fibres used in the industry as reinforcing materials for textiles. These fibres could provoke serious respiratory diseases such as byssinosis and asbestosis.

In certain textile factories the relative humidity is sometimes as high as 95 per cent with temperatures up to 35 °C. When humidity and temperatures are too high, working conditions become uncomfortable and the health and efficiency of the workers suffer. The standards of lighting in many textile industries is poor, and textile processes are also very noisy. Workers need to shout to hear each other since noise levels normally exceed 85 decibels. The use of toxic chemicals such as dyestuff can cause bladder cancer; sodium bichromate and potassium can cause chrome poisoning or chrome eczema; toxic solvents used in the finishing process for degreasing and spotting can frequently cause dermatitis and chemical poisoning from their vapours. Young workers or children are usually engaged in feeding the cloth or cotton waste into bleaching tanks and in removing it. Fatal accidents occur from exposure to chemicals, such as bleaching solutions and hot alkaline liquor, while workers are inside the tank and valves are not locked, or when another worker has opened a valve admitting one of these substances without noticing that there was someone inside. Workers can be burnt, scalded or drowned.

There is a high risk of fire due to the fact that the materials from which the textile mills are built are normally wood and other easily ignitable materials; the floor is often covered with oil that has dripped off the machines. Cotton and synthetic fibres, in particular, are highly flammable.

Carpet weaving — Carpet weaving is most common in India, Morocco and Pakistan. It is mainly a family-based industry where children also work. Most of the weavers work in rural areas, combining it with agriculture, but some are concentrated in urban looms where they depend on weaving for their living. In rural areas the work is less monotonous and it is carried out under healthier conditions than in the looms of the cities. A comparative study of 500 carpet-weaving children and 450 schoolchildren between the ages of 6 and 16, in a rural area of Kashmir,[7] has found that some of the illnesses, such as abdominal pain, diarrhoea, dysentery and fever of unknown origin, were more common in schoolchildren, and might be associated with poor sanitary, nutritional and environmental conditions of both populations. However, the height and weight of carpet-weaving children were less than those of schoolchildren; they had a higher incidence of conjunctival pallor, stomatitis, atrophic papillae and they complained about headaches, blurring of vision, backache and pain in the abdomen and limbs; they had a higher proportion of respiratory tract infections which were associated with the duration of exposure, poor lighting and bad postural conditions.

Work usually takes place in congested sheds in long rows behind big looms where the air can be thick with particles of fluff and wool. The rooms lack adequate ventilation and most of the children work in awkward positions which might hinder physical growth and development. Some of the hazards included in this type of work are visual strain and blurred vision, joint problems, intoxication from exposure to carcinogenic dyes, dermatitis, respiratory tract infections from exposure to dusts, anthrax, asthma and tuberculosis, fatigue from long hours of work (from 12 to 14 hours per day) and malnutrition. In some cases, children are also exposed to physical abuse, or are in bonded labour. Most children in these workshops are under 12 years old.[8] Carpet weavers start at an early age, due to the low cost of their labour, but they also retire early because of their working conditions.

Garment and leather industry — Fire remains one of the most serious hazards in garment shops all over the world, many of which employ large numbers of children, such as some leather tanning industries in Egypt or the garment industry in Bangladesh. Hazardous conditions such as locked or non-existent fire exits, overcrowded aisles and overloaded electrical circuits are frequent. The leather industry is a particularly hazardous area of the garment industry due to the use of solvents of high neurotoxicity and hepatotoxicity. In some shops children run sewing machines or they use punch presses to make belts. Injuries from large blades which are used to cut leather or from strong punch presses for belts are frequent. Hazards also include burns from ovens used to pleat, and industrial sewing machines which can injure fingers. Inspectors from the Apparel Industry Task Force of the New York State Department of Labor visited garment workshops in New York City, in the summer of 1988, and they found many 14-year-old children working, but there were also children as young as four years old helping their mothers to sew faster by passing material between sewing machines.[9]

Ceramics and glass factory work — Child labour in this industry is more common in Asia but can be found in other regions as well.[10] Children carry molten loads of glass, draw molten glass from tank furnaces with a temperature of 1,500 °C to 1,800 °C and carry burning hot glass from the tanks. They work in rooms with poor lighting and little or no ventilation to avoid the blow out from the flames where they join and anneal the glass bangles. The temperature inside the factories ranges from 40 °C to 45 °C and some glass factories operate only at night. Good housekeeping is lacking in these workplaces, as the floor is covered with broken glass, in many cases electric wires are exposed and no insulated internal wiring is provided. Most children, like adult workers, work 8 hours a day but they are paid only two-thirds of an adult wage. The main hazards are exposure to high temperatures leading to heat stress and cataract burns, lacerations and injuries from broken glass, hearing impairment from noise, eye injuries and eye strain from poor lighting, exposure to lead and alkaline dusts, and inhalation of toxic fumes such as carbon monoxide and sulphur dioxide. After a few years of work, most workers in this industry suffer from respiratory diseases such as asthma, bronchitis and silicosis.

Matches and fireworks industry — The production of matches normally takes place in small cottage units or in small-scale factories in a village. In some cases, children have to spend 2 to 3 hours travelling from their homes to the workplace, so special transportation is provided by the owners of the factories for this purpose. The average length of a working day can be from 10 to 12 hours, in overcrowded small rooms with poor lighting, poor sanitary conditions, no protective equipment and no medical assistance available.

In a study undertaken in India, children under 7 years of age were involved in almost all tasks in the production of matches.[11] The children were between 3 and 15 years old. Most of these industries are run on a piece-rate basis and children earn only approximately 50 per cent of what adults earn for the same tasks. Children are considered a good labour force as they work longer hours and are more dependable.

The main tasks include filling frames, making boxes, sticking labels, counting matches and dipping sticks into chemicals. The tips of the sticks are dipped into a hot solution of gum and chemicals, left to dry and then cleaned and polished. The outer striking surfaces are coated with chemicals with a brush or a roller. Nearly all workers are exposed to airborne concentrations of hazardous substances. Asbestos powder and gum arabic are used for fillers, binders, and adhesives. Potassium chlorate and antimony trisulphide are used in the fabrication of the heads of the matches. Amorphous red phosphorus mixed with sand or powdered glass is used for the friction strip. Tetraphosphorous trisulphide is used for the head of "strike anywhere" matches (i.e. matches that do not necessarily have to be lit by using the friction strip on the box). Very few units have proper ventilation. In the boiler room where the chemical gum is prepared for tipping the sticks, there is exposure to dust, fumes and vapours. The risks of fire and explosion are present all the time. As regards the fireworks units, the danger is more evident. In these units the main tasks include dyeing outer paper, stuffing the cracker powder into firecrackers, rolling gum powder and packing the final product.

There are no specific studies on the various kinds of respiratory diseases of the children working in this industry. However, as exposure to chemicals, mineral and asbestos dust, poor ventilation and overcrowding are characteristic of these workplaces, we can presume that there is a high risk of respiratory diseases, poisoning and dermatitis, and risk of burns or even death from fire or explosion.

Slate-making — Slate is a sedimentary rock which contains high concentrations of calcium carbonate, silicates, iron oxides, free silica and quartz. Slates are used in roofing; stair treads; door, window and porch casements; flooring; fireplaces; billiard tables; school blackboards; and electricity switch panels. As a powder it is used as a filler or pigment in rust proofing or insulating paints and in products for road surfacing.

Slate processing in workshops usually involves slate polishing with manual guiders or automatic polishers. There is a great danger of exposure to silicious dust from the slate particles, during drilling and polishing. The degree of dust depends on the working procedure. Long-term exposure can cause respiratory diseases such as chronic bronchitis, pneumoconiosis and emphysema. Silicotic lesions become apparent after about 10 to 15 years of exposure. As the condition does not always cause serious disability in the first years of exposure, active work is still possible for quite some time after the disease has appeared. For exposed children the symptoms may be a slight cough and chest pain. They may reach adulthood before they develop silicotic lesions.

Paint shops — During the painting process, several hazardous substances and materials are involved, such as organic solvents, binders, pigments and preservatives, asbestos, silica and lead, which are highly toxic. The most common solvents in paint and varnishes are xylene and white spirit. Some solvents and pigments contain chromates and lead. They can damage the central nervous system, cause liver injury, allergies, eczema, reproductive impairments and lung cancer. Organic solvents have allergenic, mutagenic, teratogenic and carcinogenic effects.

Child and adolescent workers exposed to these substances are house painters, car painters, varnishers, carpet-layers and wood and furniture workers. In the painting of buildings, exposure to solvents is gradual as work proceeds. It is generally done with no effective ventilation and respiratory protection, and gloves are often either not provided or not used (personal protective equipment is only designed for adults in any case and would not be suitable). The most common application methods are painting with roller and brush, high pressure spraying and in certain cases low pressure spraying. Building painters might be exposed to solvent concentrations about six times the limit threshold values (LTV). Organic solvents can be compounds within the paint or can be used to remove old paint. Silica and asbestos dust can be absorbed through sand sparkling when scraping surfaces to remove old paint. There could be exposure to leaded paint from old buildings. Among adult painters, mortality and incidence of lung cancer are significantly higher than among other working populations.

Accidental poisoning of children and adolescents with paint or solvents may generate bowel irritation with pain and diarrhoea, and gastritis with pain and vomiting. Primers based on lead are lethal if eaten by young children, and neurotoxic effects can be expected to be more dramatic due to higher concentrations of exposure and better digestive capacity.

Workers can also suffer fatigue from long hours of work; musculo-skeletal disorders such as strain on the neck, arms and shoulders are frequent due to the awkward postures they adopt while painting. As these substances are highly flammable, risks of fire and explosion also exist.

Metalwork — The welding process to render metal pliable or liquid by heat or pressure is done through a flame produced by combustion of fuel gas with air or oxygen, an electric arc (stuck between an electrode and a workpiece or between two electrodes) and electrical resistance to the passage of currents between two or more workpieces. Welding is frequently used in the toy industry, repair of batteries, auto repair stations, small electronics, and repair shops for television and domestic appliances.

Hazards from welding and flame torch fumes include exposure to extreme heat, flying sparks and hot metal objects, exposure to lead, iron, aluminium, nickel or chromium, exposure to airborne carbon monoxide and carbon dioxide, smoke and other irritants. Acute toxic effects from metals result from their inhalation in the air or their ingestion. The symptoms following the ingestion of excessive amounts of metals are those of food poisoning with nausea, vomiting, abdominal pain and in some cases diarrhoea. Chronic effects may cause severe damage to the respiratory tract with bronchitis, chemical pneumonitis and in severe cases pulmonary oedema, renal toxicity and neurological impairment.

Local exhaust ventilation, as well as respiratory protective equipment and goggles are necessary to avoid health damage. These measures are frequently not taken in the case of small welding processes, usually done by homeworkers or workers from micro-enterprises, where children and adolescents are often exposed to hazards which may result in eye injury and intoxication.

Brickmaking — Bricks and tiles made from clay have been used as building materials since the earliest times in many parts of the world. The basic material is clay with mixtures of loams, shales and sand to give the required properties of texture, pliability, shrinkage and colour according to local needs. The processing of clay includes extraction, crushing, grinding, screening and mixing. After giving it shape, it is cut to size and semi-dried before firing. Firing may take place in ring kilns, often hand fed, or in tunnel kilns mechanically fed. A finishing glaze is applied to some decorative bricks. Children may be involved in the grinding, mixing, finishing and carrying of bricks. The main hazards in this activity are: exposure to silica, carrying of excessive weights, burns from ovens, lead exposure from glaze, thermal stress due to excessive heat from ovens, carbon monoxide exposure from kilns, injuries and accidents with tools. Brickyards employing children are common in Pakistan, India, Bolivia and Colombia.

Button-making — Button-making is an important industry in many parts of the world. Modern button factories are often mechanized but where child labour is found, buttons are still produced as handicrafts; the task will be more or less complicated depending on the age of the child.

Raw material can be of natural animal, vegetable or mineral origin, or synthetic. The most frequently used raw materials are: animal origin (bone, ivory, horn, leather, mother of pearl); vegetable origin (wood, seeds of ivory palm, cellulose, linen); mineral or metal (iron, zinc, aluminium, brass, silver, gold); synthetic (polystyrene, acrylic resins, etc.); porcelain and glass.

The manufacturing process includes auto-claving, sawing, pressing and punching. In some cases, horns and hooves may be pulverized, mixed with urea-formaldehyde adhesive and moulded with a moulding press. Wooden buttons are impregnated with chemicals such as wood preservatives and dyes. Metal buttons may be pressed from steel sheets or cast in a foundry, then they will be ground and polished, painted, enamelled, electroplated and anodized. Imitation mother of pearl is obtained by use of bismuth or lead salts or aluminium powder or a product made from fish scales.

The main hazards are: machinery used with unguarded moving parts; dust exposure; risk of explosion and fire; hazardous chemical exposure if the buttons are plastic, and when solvents are used, exposure to benzene, carbon tetrachloride, pigment/dye; anthrax from bone; hearing impairment from noise; repetitive motion injuries from vibration; ocular fatigue if lighting is poor, and excessive heat.

Precious stones and gems industry — Child labour in the gem industry is widespread in India. According to the Gurupadaswany report[12] in 1979 over 13,000 children under the age of 14 were engaged in this industry, which represented approximately 20 per cent of the workforce of the industry. Precious stones are processed by hand and semi-precious stones often by machines to cut down the costs of production. Children are engaged in almost all the processing of semi-precious stones (carving, grinding and polishing). In the processing of precious stones, children are involved once the final shape and facets of the stone are cut and polished by an adult. Children have to do the final polishing by using chromic oxides which give the stones their final lustre and in cementing roughly-shaped stones or sticks.

Most of the child labour is recruited under the guise of apprenticeship training, but in fact the purpose is the provision of cheap labour. Children begin to work at the age of 6 or 7 years doing small tasks including domestic work. During this period the child does not get paid; occasionally a few rupees and food are provided to keep his or her interest. Most of these children are completely illiterate and work approximately 10 hours a day. After 3 to 4 years the child has started to learn to make more facets, and starts getting paid by the age of 15 years old. By this age the child has learnt most of the finer polishing techniques and will receive half of the salary that an adult worker will get. At that age a child can do about 30 per cent more work than an adult.

The work is carried out mainly in small workshops which usually have a poor working environment. The main hazards in this industry are: eye strain due to poor lighting, musculo-skeletal disorders from bad sitting postures, small wounds on the hands, large knots at the base of the fingers grazed by the cutting discs, poisoning and dermatitis from exposure to oxides and poor ventilation and sanitation. Some of the oxides used in this industry are aluminium oxide, ceric oxide, chromic oxide, ferric oxide, silica dioxide, stannic oxide and zirconium dioxide, which are mixed with water and used for grinding and polishing.

Abattoirs and meat processing

An abattoir is a slaughterhouse for animals intended for human consumption such as horned cattle, pigs, sheep and in some countries horses and camels. The abattoir may be a self-contained unit existing solely for the supply of meat for sale to butchers' shops, or it may be part of a large factory in which the meat is processed. Small abattoirs are found in rural areas. They are often housed in inadequate buildings with primitive equipment. As the number of workers employed will normally be small, they will be involved in all the operational processes, which include the slaughter of animals, cutting of carcasses, removal of inedible parts and of hair and skin of dead animals, carrying carcasses, use of water-heating vessels and exposure to extreme temperature changes. Most of the tasks children carry out are to assist adult workers in the slaughter of animals and the removal and carrying of carcasses.

As the sanitary conditions are usually poor, liquid and solid wastes can provoke falls due to slippery floors. As waste is often left untreated, this results in bad smells and attracts rats and flies which breed in large quantities. Sharp blades of power saws can amputate limbs or cause severe lacerations and eye injuries from flying bone chips. Repetitive strain injuries and musculo-skeletal disorders can occur from the heavy weight of large pieces of meat; puncture wounds are frequent with risks of infection; the manipulation of sick animals can provoke Q fever, brucellosis, tuberculosis and other infectious diseases; and thermal stress and respiratory diseases are frequent.

Deep-sea diving/fishing

Deep-sea diving is common in Asia, particularly in the Philippines, Indonesia, Thailand and Burma.[13] Muro-ami is a fishing method that relies on swimming children who beat on coral reefs to scare the fish into nets. Each fishing ship employs up to 300 boys between the ages of 10 and 15 recruited from poor neighbourhoods.

Divers reset the net several times a day, therefore children are in the water for up to 12 hours. Dozens of young swimmers die or get injured each year. They can be attacked by predatory fish (needlefish, sharks, barracudas, poisonous sea-snakes) or suffer from decompression illness or accidents due to hypoxia from exposure to high atmospheric pressure. They are exposed to gastro-intestinal and other communicable diseases on board the vessels, which are congested and have poor sanitary conditions.

Services sector

Large numbers of children are increasingly being employed in this sector all over the world. Children can be found working in restaurants, hotels, garages, shops, etc., as labourers, servants, maids, cooks, waiters, bartenders, shop assistants, and as messengers. Most of the time, they work long hours, are low paid and in some cases have to carry heavy loads; often they have no sanitary facilities or rest areas.

Bakeries — The main hazards include: exposure to machines with unguarded heavy blades; cutting blades and rollers when mixing, kneading and beating dough; burns from hot ovens; carrying heavy weights, risk of explosion of ovens; risks of laceration with knives and from wrapping materials; dermatitis from exposure to flour, plastic gloves or frequent hand-washing; noise; eye injuries from ultraviolet bactericidal lamps in fermenting processes; thermal stress and electrocutions.

Grocery stores/supermarkets — The most frequent hazards include: cuts with slicers, lacerations, falls from heights, falls on slippery floors, hits and injuries by falling objects and carrying heavy loads. There are traffic hazards if delivery is included, especially if delivery is timed. In many countries in Latin America, child packers do not receive a salary and they survive on tips from the clients.

Auto-repair garages and petrol stations — Garages are a widespread source of employment in which older children and young persons are involved, particularly in Africa and Latin America. A diversity of tasks are carried out such as housing or parking of vehicles, supply of motor fuel and maintenance services such as washing, tyre pressure maintenance, electrical or mechanical repairs including painting and surface treatment of metal.

A garage can be a very small undertaking with the proprietor working alongside a limited number of employees. In the informal sector, it can be just an open area with or without a roof. Older children can be found in apprenticeships. Due to the variety of activities and equipment, there is a wide range of risks. The most common hazards include: poisoning from exposure to benzene, leaded petrol, diesel, carbon monoxide, rubber adhesives and solvents used in vulcanization; exposure to asbestos fibres from brake and clutch lining repairs and disc dressing; dermatitis and chemical poisoning from acids and metals from batteries and from epoxy resins used in lacquers and reactive agents in glues; burns from hot water in radiator repairs and on hot engine parts; falls and injuries from bad housekeeping, storage and maintenance of equipment; poor ventilation in confined spaces; lack of protective clothing and equipment; inadequate sanitary and washing facilities, risk of fire and explosion by accidental ignition of gasoline vapour; injuries by lifting machinery with defective chains or by falls of vehicles in the elevator or from jacks.

Marginal productive activities

Domestic service/housework — As children are not supposed to be working for a salary, most working children at high risk are often inaccessible, as they are concentrated in occupations where they are out of sight from possible observers. Children in domestic service often suffer from physical and sexual abuse. This situation is reinforced by the fact that households are not considered workplaces and authorities are not entitled to enter the premises to investigate labour abuses.

The number of children occupied as domestic servants working and living away from home represents a large percentage of those involved in the informal sector, most of them being girls. The limited available information shows that they work very long hours, under psychological pressure, in almost total isolation from their family and friends. For example, according to a recent survey carried out in Colombia, domestic servants under 15 years of age worked an average of 50 hours a week. Girl domestic servants constituted the majority of all children working very long hours each day.[14] There is also alarming evidence of physical, mental and sexual abuse of adolescents and young women working as household helpers or child-minders.

A survey on household helpers carried out in Nairobi by the WHO showed that out of 500 domestic servants between the ages of 6 and 15 years of age, 90 per cent suffered from severe emotional distress, symptoms of withdrawal and regression, premature ageing, depression, and low self-esteem.[15] Most of these children had sleeping problems, exhibited phobic reactions to their employers, wet their beds and in some cases behaved older than their chronological age. They suffered from separation from their families and were generally mistreated by their employers, being beaten or sexually abused. The main tasks were kitchen work, cleaning residences, washing and ironing, and outside errands.

Hazards in this sector include: physical and sexual abuse; malnutrition; excessive hours of work; child-raising responsibilities despite still being children themselves; heavy loads (lifting other children, household goods and food) leading to back problems; knee problems (bursitis, tendinitis) from cleaning on their knees; burns; scalds; and dermatitis from washing clothes by hand, with drastic changes from hot to cold.

Home work — Hazards will depend on what is being made at home. Such work may include sewing, electronics assembly, jewellery or toy-making. Known hazards include fatigue from night work, lead exposure and chemical exposure in the assembly of electronic appliances.

Toy making — Toy making is one of the most frequent types of home work, and it can also be carried out in micro-enterprises within the informal sector. It is particularly frequent in Thailand and the Philippines. The process of toy manufacturing will vary according to local practice and the raw materials from which the articles are made. Raw materials most commonly used are: ferrous materials, wood, plastic, fabric, paper and cardboard, stuffing materials such as sawdust, polyurethane foam, wool, cotton and rags, paints, solvents and adhesives. This type of work, when done by children, can be carried out in small workshops or may be given out to homeworkers.

There is a high risk of fire from many of the materials used, like cellulose, plastic and stuffing materials. The exposed moving parts of the machinery and tools used can cause injuries. Burns can be caused by contact or spillage where hot processes, acids or caustic soda are involved. Where electroplating is involved, there is risk of poisoning by the inhalation of metal vapours. When using chemicals such as paint, solvents and adhesives there is also risk of intoxication. Chrome ulcers and dermatitis can develop from contact with chromic acid. There is risk of lead poisoning where lead or lead alloys are used.

Scavenging in dumps/rag-picking — This is more frequent in big cities in developing countries such as Brazil, Mexico, the Philippines and Thailand.

Children engaged in this type of activity live in conditions of extreme poverty and deprivation. They make their living by picking up and selling used paper, plastic, bottles, metal pieces, tins, rags, clothes and other objects from street garbage or dump sites. They carry out their tasks in a highly unhealthy and dangerous working environment where they are exposed to infectious diseases including hepatitis A and B, AIDS/HIV, tetanus and coliform. Children are at risk of laceration from glass and sharp metal. They are exposed to toxic fumes and volatile compounds from burning plastic or other materials with possible risk of respiratory impairments or residual long-term asthma. While working in the dumps they are often at risk of being run over by large machines such as bulldozers or dump-trucks, or being buried and suffocated by garbage. There is also the risk of thermal stress and burns. Food poisoning and other digestive disorders from eating left-over food are frequent. Often these children lack access to health care services.

In an ILO study on scavenger children in the Philippines, among other disorders were found: high levels of lead and mercury in blood; battering and gunshot wounds; tetanus; impaired lung function, ubiquitous presence of parasites; skin disorders and other conditions associated with a poorly controlled and dangerous working environment.[16]

Street work — In street trades, the most frequent hazards are rather associated with children having to work in the street than with the activity they undertake, unless it is related to drug carriers or prostitution. For those children selling goods in the street, there is a risk of being run over or hit by cars, exposure to heat, noise, cold and dust; exposure to carbon monoxide from the fuel of vehicles, falls from bicycles, head injuries, exposure to violence and criminal activities.[17] Often children who live in the street are intimately linked to the illicit drug industry; they are used in the production and marketing of cocaine and in the trafficking of cannabis and heroin. In some cases, they are exploited by terrorists and criminal organizations and recruited to carry out subversive and criminal activities. According to a study carried out by the WHO Programme on Substance Abuse,[18] among street children in 10 cities around the world (Alexandria, Bombay, Cairo, Lusaka, Manila, Mexico City, Montreal, Rio de Janeiro, Tegucigalpa and Toronto), a significant proportion of street children regularly consume alcohol and other drugs. The more widely used are those that are cheap and easily available such as alcohol, tobacco, cannabis, glue, solvents, amphetamines and other pharmaceuticals. However, the consumption of cocaine, heroin and a combination of new drugs is increasing.

Slavery and bonded labour

Slavery is still a widespread phenomenon in the world. Child slavery predominates in those social systems that are based on the exploitation of poverty, such as debt bondage incurred by a family. War, migration and the consequential break-up of family structures also contribute to child slavery. Available information shows the existence of traditional forms of child slavery in South Asia and in the sub-Saharan strip of East Africa. Similar cases have also been found in two Latin American countries. Contemporary forms of child slavery seem to be evolving all over the world, either by a link established between an adult's work contract which allows for exercising rights of temporary or permanent ownership over the child or by the exchange of a child for an amount of money which is often described as an advance on wages. The owner can have the child working directly for him or her, or rent the child's services to a third party.

According to the report of the ILO Committee of Experts on the Application of Conventions and Recommendations to the International Labour Conference Session of 1990,[19] more than 30 million children were in slavery or bondage in several countries, including Brazil, the Dominican Republic, Ghana, Haiti, India, Mauritania, Pakistan, Peru, the Philippines, South Africa and Thailand. Of these children, over 10 million were concentrated in India and Pakistan.

Family bondage in rural areas is the most common arrangement and consists of debt bondage where children work with their family to help repay a loan. They are obliged to provide free labour for an indefinite period of time, remaining bound in a lifetime contract through generations, as it is impossible for the loan to be paid off. Another frequent type of arrangement is when the child is sold by the parents for a sum of money or for the payment of a family debt, to be used as captive workforce. Most of these children are abused both mentally and physically. They can be found working in plantations, in small workshops from the informal sector in carpet weaving, in match factories, in glass factories, in brickmaking, in fish cleaning, in mines and quarries; working as domestic help, engaged in the sex industry and as drug carriers.

Prostitution

There is a large number of children involved in the sex industry, particularly in prostitution, many of them in bonded labour or kidnapped. The exact number of children engaged in prostitution is unknown. According to available estimates, there are at least one million child prostitutes under the age of 18 worldwide and probably very many more, the majority of them concentrated in Asia, where the buying and selling of children has become big business. For example, child prostitution remains a widespread practice in Thailand despite the government's efforts to eliminate its occurrence. Estimates of children involved vary from 20,000 to 800,000.[20] According to the Centre for the Protection of Children's Rights in Bangkok, there are hundreds of thousands of child prostitutes in Thailand alone, many of them sold into bondage by their parents from the northern hill tribes of the country or from neighbouring countries such as the Lao People's Democratic Republic, Cambodia and China. The Foundation for Women and Friends of Women does not consider this estimation to be unrealistic, taking into account the increase in the number of indirect sex venues in which children are employed as sex workers under the façade of other activity.[21]

Children engaged in prostitution are at serious risk to their physical and mental well-being and also in danger of violent death. They are frequently kept in slavery conditions. With the worldwide spread of AIDS they are at a higher risk, as they are considered to be safer sex partners and this situation has stimulated the demand for younger children. The most severe health risks are AIDS/HIV and death; there are also risks of other sexually transmitted diseases (STDs) and internal damage resulting from early and unwanted teenage pregnancies with associated risks. This situation could become a major public health problem in the future, and hence is an incentive to governments to enforce laws against it.

NOTES

[1] Pollack et al., 1990a; Cogbill et al., 1985; Doyle and Conroy, 1989; Nagi, 1972; Pollack, 1990b.

[2] Wilks, 1993.

[3] For further discussion on the matter, see Annex III on chemical exposure and Annex I on the effects of work on the health status of working children.

[4] Jeyaratnam, 1985 and 1992; Jeyaratnam and Chia (eds.), 1994.

[5] WHO, 1993a.

[6] ILO, 1996.

[7] Mattoo et al., 1986.

[8] Mitra, 1991; Anti-Slavery Society, 1978 and 1988.

[9] Pollack et al., 1990b.

[10] Rastogi et al., 1989; Gupta et al., 1984.

[11] Kothari, 1983.

[12] Quoted in Burra, 1988; and in Gupta, 1989.

[13] Rialp, 1993.

[14] Kneel, 1995.

[15] WHO, 1987a.

[16] Rosario, 1988; Department of Labor and Employment (Philippines)/ILO, 1987.

[17] Mouli et al., 1991; Myers, 1989.

[18] WHO, 1993b.

[19] ILO, 1990a.

[20] ECPAT, 1995.

[21] Wanjiku Kaime-Atterhög et al., 1994.

Annex III

Chemical exposure

Children have different structural and functional characteristics from those of young people and adults, which represent stages in normal growth and development. As the process of growth and development may be modified by exposure to chemicals, all these characteristics must be taken into account in the evaluation of health risks from chemicals and other hazardous agents in children. Studies on chemical exposure in children are limited and most of them concern infants and young children (up to 5 years of age). However, based on available information, the pathways of exposure of certain chemicals in relation to growth and development are discussed in this section.

Most organs and systems of the body have not reached structural or functional maturity at birth. There is a rapid growth and development of the body as a whole and of the organs and tissues, particularly during the first 6 months of life, and it continues at a variable pace until adolescence is completed. Many organs and tissues mature at different rates, for example, the development of the nervous system continues in postnatal life and much of the myelinization of the brain takes place after birth; the structural development of the lung continues with an increase in alveolar surface area during childhood. Several components of the immune system are not fully developed at birth (for example, the lymphocytes responsible for producing antibodies). It has been suggested by some authors that this can be the cause of a greater susceptibility by newborn and infant children to certain bacterial infections.[1] The gastro-intestinal, endocrine and reproductive systems and the renal function are also immature at birth.

A chemical introduced into the body of an infant or a young child may affect the structural and functional development of a particular organ or system, which may in turn interfere with the growth and development of the body as a whole. The toxic effect of chemicals may be different at different stages of development. Some chemicals are capable of accumulating in the body tissue in greater amounts during infancy, rather than later in childhood and in adolescence when growth is slower. Moreover, chemicals reaching the body early in life may produce delayed effects in later years. The exposure of the child to chemicals can give rise not only to immediate effects, but also to manifestations in later years, due to the disturbed maturation of organ systems and their altered response to other environmental influences. Depending on the chemical concerned, the vulnerability of the developing organ systems can be higher or lower than that of more mature systems. Because the effects of the chemical may not be expressed immediately, but be delayed for some years, the health of adults may also be endangered by chemical exposure at an early stage of life. The ability to eliminate substances from the body is also important and there is the added possibility that the chemical absorbed may itself hinder growth.[2]

The variations that exist in the health and nutritional status of children from different social and cultural environments may influence exposure and modify response to chemicals. The nature and extent of exposure will be determined by the physiological, behavioural, social, cultural and occupational conditions of the family and the child; the quality of care and supervision which will be modified by social, cultural and economic factors; and the inherent behavioural patterns of the child. Special behavioural characteristics of young children can determine a greater exposure to chemicals. The response of the growing infant to a chemical may, therefore, be different from that of the fully grown adult. Recognition of this condition will help in the identification of children at risk and enable appropriate preventive and remedial measures to be adopted.

Pathways of exposure

Chemicals may enter the body of the child through the alimentary tract, the respiratory tract or the skin. Absorption depends on the physical and chemical characteristics of the chemical agent, its concentration gradient, the conditions at the site of absorption and the biological characteristics of the absorptive surface. These last two will change with age. The relative importance of the routes of absorption will vary with age according to the nature of the diet, the behavioural characteristics and the maturation of the system involved. Information is limited about age-related differences in the accumulation and elimination of chemicals. However, a greater proportion of a similar dose of a chemical per unit body weight is likely to accumulate in the body of the child, and the concentration of the chemical in the blood and tissues of the child is also likely to be higher for a similar exposure.[3]

The bio-transformation and excretion of toxins depends on the enzyme activity and the changes of the hepatic and renal functions during childhood. The maturation of the major hepatic enzymes occurs before the first year of life, therefore according to some authors, immature enzyme systems are unlikely to constitute a risk for children. A child's kidneys may be immature in some aspects as compared with an adult. According to an IPCS (International Programme on Chemical Safety) Meeting of Experts, the kidneys of an infant are immature and may be less able to excrete chemicals. A greater proportion of a similar dose of a chemical per unit body weight is likely to accumulate in the body of the infant, and the concentration of the chemical in the blood and the tissue is also likely to be higher; this will also vary with the age of the child.[4] However, according to some authors, this immaturity does not preclude their ability to excrete chemicals. In general terms, children before adolescence have higher rates of total body clearance than adults, which suggest that children will remove toxic chemicals from their bodies faster than adults, although malnutrition may increase the risk of toxicity.[5] It should be noted that in the scientific community, the response of children to toxic substances is still the subject of debate and research.

Children have a different body composition from adults. The percentage of water in the organs and tissues, and in the body as a whole, decreases with age. Most of the cells of the organs and tissues in children are smaller than in adults, therefore they have a larger surface area in relation to mass than bigger cells and bodies. For example, the femur in particular seems to have a rate of deposition of magnesium, calcium, sodium and metals, as well as chemicals present in bone, which is greater in later childhood than in infancy and decreases with age.[6]

Because of their rapid growth, children have a higher metabolic rate and oxygen consumption, and therefore a greater intake of air per unit body weight. The absorption of fumes, gases and particles depends primarily on ventilation. Children tend to be very active and to expend a lot of physical energy; they tend to breathe at a higher rate and more deeply than adults and therefore take in larger quantities of dust or vapours through the airways. It also has to be considered that resistance to toxic agents may be lowered by the increased energy expenditure required for growth. The volume of air passing through the lungs of the resting infant is twice that of the resting adult (per unit body weight) and therefore twice as much of any chemical in the atmosphere would reach the lungs of the child as compared to that reaching the lungs of the adult (per unit body weight) in the same period of time. Children between 8 and 10 years of age doing exercise have a ventilation rate 3 times higher than adults doing light work. Therefore working children may absorb larger amounts of airborne toxins than adults.[7]

Limited information is available concerning the absorption of inhaled chemical atmospheric pollutants in relation to the continuing development of the respiratory tract. However, as chemicals are absorbed more readily by the child than by the adult, exposure of infants and children to atmospheric pollutants may be enhanced compared with that of adults, when the source of emission is close to the ground and under circumstances in which gases or vapours of high density are involved. Children exposed to air polluted with sulphur dioxide, nitrogen dioxide, carbon monoxide and dust have higher rates of respiratory diseases than adults, as well as significant changes in physical development as compared with non-exposed children. Food and beverages can also be sources of exposure. Numerous examples of contamination through residues of pesticides, antibiotics, fungicides and heavy metals have been encountered as a result of agricultural techniques, veterinary practice and the use of contaminated land and water.

Infants and young children have greater energy and fluid requirements per unit body weight than adults. They have also special dietary needs, including the dependence of the infant on milk. For example, an infant living on milk needs about one seventh of his or her own weight of water each day which would correspond to 10 litres for a 70 kg man. This larger intake is necessary for infants, because they lose more water per kilo body weight through the lungs, due to the greater passage of air through them, through the skin, because of a larger surface area, and through the kidneys, because of the inability to concentrate the urine to the same extent as an older child or an adult. Therefore, the absorption of any chemical will be taken by the infant in greater quantities per unit body weight than by an older child or adult using the same water supply.

Children have a larger body surface area in relation to weight, therefore the area of the skin that could be exposed to a chemical is 2.5 times greater per unit body weight in a naked child than in a naked adult. The skin is a complex structure, the functional development of which is completed only after puberty. There will be age-related differences in the response of the skin to chemicals. For example, according to some authors, in infants and children the relatively large surface area of the skin per body weight ratio may result in greater tissue concentrations than in the adult,[8] even though there is little evidence that the rate of absorption varies with age, as the thickness of the skin is relatively constant after birth. Furthermore, different processes of absorption have been observed in children, with marked variations in absorption rates between closely related chemical compounds. Skin absorption of certain hazardous substances such as lead is also considered to be higher by some authors due to the relatively thinner dermis and epidermis.[9] According to other authors, in the case of older children physiological differences are relatively small and are not likely to have major effects on the distribution of a toxic chemical.[10] However, percutaneous absorption is enhanced when the skin is damaged or macerated. The cutaneous manifestations of a disease also vary with age, and some disorders are confined to infants and children.

The brain of the infant at birth is not fully developed. The full number of neurones is reached around 2 years of age; however, myelinization is not completed until adolescence. Based on experimental data, it has been found that there are changes in the sensitivity of the brain of animals to hormones or drugs during development and hence normal development can be hindered. No data are available on infants and children, and many co-variables have to be taken into account such as socio-economic status, nutrition and mental stimulation, in order to evaluate the effects of a chemical in the functioning of the human brain during development and to have a valid interpretation of the observations.

Data on the toxic effects of chemicals in humans are frequently incomplete or even absent, particularly in the case of infants and children; most of the examples given show that exposure to certain chemicals during postnatal development can be associated with dose-effect and dose-response relationships that differ from those resulting from exposure in later years. Therefore, any assessment of human risk on the basis of such studies should take into consideration the differences that exist between animal species used in experiments and humans in their reaction to chemicals. The conditions under which the animal data were obtained may not reflect the human circumstances of exposure.

Concerning cancer, an inherent problem in the study of postnatal exposure to carcinogens is the capacity for metabolic activation in the tissues of the newborn and infant organisms as compared with that of the adult. The perinatal development of different organs varies considerably among species. All these variables make extrapolation from animals to humans extremely difficult. No epidemiological observations on human infants have been reported in which the occurrence of cancer was associated exclusively with exposure to carcinogens in the early postnatal period. The few existing data come from animal studies.

Examples of exposure to hazardous substances and their effects on health

Carbon disulphide — Carbon disulphide is a highly toxic substance which can be found in several processes as it is contained in solvents, halogens, rubber, phosphorus, and used in the manufacture of organic chemicals such as agrochemicals, oils and resins, paints, fuels, explosives, viscose and rayon. It may also be present in small quantities in crude petroleum and coal tar. Skin absorption is possible from direct contact with liquid carbon disulphide. However, it is absorbed mainly by inhalation as a vapour. The human body retains about 40-50 per cent of the inhaled quantity of carbon disulphide; approximately 80-90 per cent of it is metabolized and can have serious neurotoxic effects. Repeated exposure to high concentrations may result in serious damage to many other body systems.

Acute poisoning is associated with psychological and behavioural changes including extreme irritability, hallucinations, manic delirium and paranoia. In adult workers long-term exposure to low concentrations may have gastrointestinal effects such as dyspepsia, gastritis and ulcerative changes; cardiovascular effects including development of coronary heart diseases; metabolic and endocrinological effects such as alteration of thyroid functions, reduction in the activity of adrenal glands, chronic nephritic and nephrotic syndromes; reproductive impairments such as spermatogenesis impairment and impotence in adult male workers; and disturbance of the hormonal balance including spontaneous abortions in adult female workers. Carbon disulphide passes through the placenta so its concentration in the tissues of the foetus is the same as in the mother. Behavioural, neurological and vascular changes may last for several years after cessation of exposure and in some cases may be permanent.

Although the existence of a particular sensitivity in children has not been studied, exposure to this highly toxic substance should be avoided, as children are likely to be particularly sensitive to respiratory irritants, and the effects of the substance on their endocrine system and their nervous system can have severe consequences on their growth and development.

Benzene — Benzene is used in the manufacture of organic chemicals, pesticides, detergents and paint removers, and it is also used as a solvent. Liquid benzene has a defatting effect on the skin and direct contact with it may cause dermatitis. Variations exist in individual sensitivity to acute or chronic poisoning, apparently explained, among other factors, by variations in the extent of fatty tissues. High concentrations of benzene vapour cause narcotic effects and slight irritation to the eyes and mucous membranes of the respiratory tract. In adult workers acute poisoning has severe narcotic effects that could provoke coma and death due to respiratory arrest. Chronic poisoning caused by long-term exposure to lower concentrations of benzene may, in particular, result in bone marrow suppression and leukaemia. However, there may be a latent period of several years between the cessation of the exposure to benzene and the onset of leukaemia. Children are generally more sensitive than adults to this substance.

Lead and other metals — Children constitute the group at the greatest risk of lead poisoning. Metals are retained in the brain more readily in infancy than in adulthood. This has been discussed extensively in the case of lead.[11] Infants and children absorb substantially more lead than adults. Lead may affect the metabolization of vitamin D; it can also interfere in skeletal development. The concentration of lead in human bones doubles between infancy and late adolescence.[12] Absorption from the gastrointestinal tract is particularly efficient in young children. Organic lead compounds, such as tetraethyl lead, can be absorbed through the skin, but inorganic lead cannot. In the past decade, scientific advances in the epidemiology of environmental lead exposure in children have led to the recognition of a syndrome of silent lead toxicity, in which children may suffer serious damage from exposure to lead without having overt symptoms. The toxic effects of different levels of lead exposure range from mild inhibition of certain enzymes to an acute encephalopathy which is characterized by lack of coordination, confusion, swelling of the brain and seizures, and it may induce epilepsy, coma or even death.

For each kilogram of body weight, children eat more and breathe a greater volume of air. Because of this, lead levels rise more in children than in adults in response to an increase in ingestion or respiration of airborne lead levels. The metabolism of lead also differs between children and adults. A young person's absorption of lead from the stomach and intestines is more efficient, especially in the presence of certain nutritional deficiencies (e.g. iron, calcium or zinc), which are fairly common among poor children and might provoke impaired growth and development.

From the total lead amount in a child's body, a greater proportion is metabolically active than the portion stored in bones. Lead toxicity in an adult shows up primarily as peripheral nervous system dysfunction (e.g. muscle weakness). Lead effects in children usually involve the central nervous system. The nervous system of a child during its development is especially vulnerable, as the brain and blood cells that protect the brain from contact with toxic substances circulating in the blood are not completely developed. Furthermore, the faster rate of cellular metabolism of the immature brain makes it more vulnerable than the adult brain to the adverse effects of lead on cell respiration and oxygen transportation. Excessive exposure to lead in the critical stages of development may alter the number and connections between nerve cells, possibly resulting in irreversible changes in the brain structure and function.

In studies carried out in Australia, Belgium, Denmark, Germany, Greece, Italy, Mexico, the United Kingdom, the United States and the former Yugoslavia,[13] it has been found that signs of peripheral nervous system dysfunction (slower reaction time, slower nerve-conduction velocity and abnormalities in brain waves reflected in electro-encephalograms) were evident at levels below 30 µg/dl (microgrammes per decilitre). Apparently there is a remarkably small margin of safety between "average" lead exposure levels and those considered hazardous. Children do not have to work near a lead smelter or a hazardous waste dump to accumulate unhealthy amounts of lead in the system; it is enough to live nearby. The blood levels near or even below 25 µg/dl impair the function of children's blood-forming organs, the endocrine system (including vitamins and calcium metabolism), overall growth and intellectual development. Other deficits linked to levels comparable to or below those presently considered toxic were: lower reading achievement, hearing impairment, below normal stature and poor classroom behaviour for those children attending school (e.g. inattentiveness, inability to follow directions, impulsiveness, physical aggression).

Concerning subclinical exposure to lead, even if most public health experts support the hypothesis that subclinical lead exposure produces cognitive impairment in children, there is an ongoing debate over the magnitude of lead's impact on intellectual functioning and the conditions under which that impact is apparent. This is due to the fact that it is difficult to demonstrate that the intellectual deficiencies observed in these children are actually caused by lead exposure, or that there is a combination of factors such as poor health, inadequate nutrition, or a lack of medical care and educational opportunities. In order to establish with greater certainty which comes first — lead exposure or intellectual impairment — recent studies have begun testing children at or prior to birth. The tests measure blood-lead level and various indexes of mental functioning over a period of time. In addition to clarifying the issue of causation, these studies are generating a wealth of new information about the impact of foetal lead exposure on a child's early development.

Other sources of lead exposure include the refining of jewellery waste to recover gold, and the reconditioning and smelting of lead-containing batteries to obtain scrap lead, both of which are common sources of childhood plumbism in Sri Lanka.[14] Burning lead-containing batteries for cooking purposes or to provide heat have also caused lead poisoning in children in poor communities. Agrochemicals containing lead derivatives can also be highly toxic. The epilepsy epidemic in the Lakhumpur Kherii district of India has been attributed to the toxicity of the pesticide benzene hexachloride which is used as food grain preservative.[15] For children who work in old buildings or structures with poor ventilation, buildings painted with leaded paint could be sources of hazardous lead exposure; for those involved in the painting of buildings during wall renovations in which lead-painted surfaces are disturbed, sanding and scraping liberates large amounts of very small lead particles that are difficult to enclose and are readily inhaled or ingested.

Leaded petrol provokes the dispersion of enormous amounts of lead into the environment through internal combustion engines using this fuel. Airborne lead derived from the combustion of leaded petrol provides at least 25 per cent of an individual's exposure. Airborne lead continues to be an important source of exposure for children working in the streets of big cities due to the petrol fumes from vehicles and for those working or living near lead smelters or other industrial sources.

Excessive exposure to selenium during the development of the teeth might increase susceptibility to caries. Methyl mercury is also well-absorbed and, as it is more likely to be retained in children than in adults, it can provoke impaired neurological and mental development.[16] The liver and kidneys also accumulate metals, as do other tissues that take up metals more easily in the early period of life, when growth is rapid, than when growth has slowed down or ceased.

Mercury — This is a silvery liquid metal with a melting point of −39°C. It evaporates at room temperatures. It is used in a variety of compounds, both inorganic (oxides, chlorides, nitrates and sulphates) and organic (alkyl and aryl). Metallic mercury is used in several processes, such as in the production and repair of electrical measuring devices, fluorescent lamps, in some paints, dyes, textiles and jewellery, and in the paper industry. It is also found in many types of occupations, particularly in mercury-ore mining. In agriculture mercury chloride is used as a fungicide for treating bulbs and protecting wood. Aryl and alkyl mercury compounds are used as fungicides or as disinfectants; seed treatment and wood protection are carried out with organic compounds of mercury. Occupational exposure to the vapours of elemental mercury is the main hazard. It enters into the body through the lungs as vapour or dust and about 80 per cent of the inhaled vapours are absorbed. Metallic mercury is absorbed by ingestion from the digestive tract only in small amounts through water-soluble mercury compounds. Some organic and inorganic mercury compounds may be absorbed through the skin. The effects of mercury are highly variable: inorganic mercury poisoning is primarily renal; elemental and organic mercury poisoning is primarily neurological; exposure to inorganic mercury vapour may irreversibly damage the central nervous system; accidental ingestion of inorganic mercury salts, such as mercury chloride, causes local necrosis in the mouth and digestive tract, circulatory collapse and acute failure of kidneys, with oliguria and anuria. Mercury compounds of low solubility in water usually have low toxicity. Chronic poisoning due to mercury vapour includes erethism, tremor and stomatitis.

There is no data on child exposure, even if children engaged in mercury-ore mining have been recorded. However, available clinical data on adult workers do not permit extensive conclusions about the dose-response relationship concerning airborne mercury exposure, because there is no substantial accumulation of evidence or any conclusive report about the incidence of poisoning at exposure concentrations below 0.01 mg/m³ of mercury in air. In adult workers, short-term exposure to metallic mercury vapour at concentrations in the range of 1-3 mg/m³ of air causes acute poisoning, such as irritation of the bronchial mucous membranes, stomatitis and pneumonitis. According to the WHO's maximum tolerable dose (MTD) in adult workers, concentrations of metallic and inorganic mercury of 0.05 mg/m³ and less are not believed to lead to intoxication if adult workers are exposed 8 hours a day, 5 days a week.[17]

In adult workers, neurological and psychological damage can have non-specific early symptoms such as anorexia, weight loss and headaches, followed by more characteristic disorders such as increased irritability, sleep disturbance, excitability, anxiety, depression, memory defects and loss of self-confidence.

Organic solvents — Organic solvents are volatile compounds used for dissolving materials which are not soluble in water, such as fats, waxes and resins, mixtures for paint, varnishes and other chemical products. They are frequently used in agriculture and in the plastic, printing, graphics, metal, textile and dry-cleaning industries, including those processes where workers manufacture or use adhesives, lacquers and paints. Due to the increased use of chemicals in different work processes, millions of workers in the world are potentially exposed daily to organic solvents by inhalation, skin contact or ingestion. Their most frequent uses are in painting, thinning and cleaning. Even if they are chemically heterogeneous, these compounds are grouped because they have similar toxicologic effects. The main ones are: benzene, toluene, xylene, dioxane, trichloroethylene, ethylene glycol ethers, ketone, carbon tetrachlorides, carbon disulphide, methylene chloride and methyl chloroform.

The magnitude of the adverse health effects due to organic solvents is unknown and depends on the intensity and duration of the exposure. Minor exposure to organic solvents irritates the eyes and the mucous membrane of the nose and throat, and can cause allergies. They also affect the skin, causing dermatitis. Organic solvents can also cause neurological damage and death.

Most reports on solvent-related encephalopathy describe long-term exposure or short-term exposure to very high concentrations associated with loss of consciousness. With acute exposure, the symptoms can range from lethargy to unconsciousness and to death, according to the degree of exposure. Low chronic exposure symptoms are irritability, fatigue, difficulty in concentration and loss of interest. Chronic exposure provokes renal toxicity and neural-behavioural effects, such as changes in personality or intellectual functions and global deterioration of the cognitive functions.

Prolonged exposure to an elevated concentration in the air can cause permanent damage to the central nervous system. However, most of the information on their neurotoxicity derives from animal studies. Some organic solvents are also suggested to be teratogenic and carcinogenic to humans. There is evidence that exposure in adult female workers can cause spontaneous abortions and congenital malformations.

Even if there are no specific studies on children's exposure to most of the substances described above, due to the highly toxic effects of these substances, children should not be exposed to them. As mentioned in the second part of this publication, occupational exposure limits for adult workers do not apply to children. Limit values for the public should be used in their case.

NOTES

[1] IPCS, 1986.

[2] Idem.

[3] The same difference exists between infants, young children and older children. Therefore age plays an important role in determining the consequence of exposure.

[4] IPCS, 1986.

[5] McGuigan, 1994.

[6] For a more detailed discussion on the rate of deposition in bones according to age, see IPCS, 1986.

[7] McGuigan, 1994.

[8] Wester and Maibach, 1982.

[9] Berger et al., 1991.

[10] McGuigan, 1994; Reed and Besunder, 1989.

[11] United Kingdom Department of Heath and Social Security, 1980.

[12] Barry, 1975.

[13] Bellinger, 1991.

[14] Senanayake and Román, 1993.

[15] ibid.

[16] Amin-Zaki et al., 1976.

[17] WHO, 1986a.

Annex IV

Expert system for the identification of occupational diseases in clinical and surveillance applications[1]

An example of a useful structure for the collection of data is the establishment of an expert system. An **expert system** has two major components: the **knowledge database structure** (factual data) and the **method** employed by the expert to use the knowledge database. The knowledge database structure provides insight into the types of information used by occupational medicine for reaching a diagnosis. Its content is based on clinical practice and a review of technical literature. A general structure should be developed. The structure of the knowledge database includes general information which is necessary to make it diagnostically useful.

The structure of an **expert system knowledge database** includes the following components:

(a)   factual knowledge;

(b)   input and output requirements;

(c)   algorithm for reaching diagnoses;

(d)   specification of uncertainties; and

(e)   recognition of diagnostic "biases".

Factual knowledge

The first component of the system's structure includes general categories of information: occupation, industry, exposure to agents, diseases and the relation among these categories. This structure also permits the inclusion of information about estimated frequency of exposure, e.g. how many children working in a particular activity or task have actually been exposed, and what the level of exposure is among those who are exposed. Frequency and magnitude of exposure among those actually exposed also require specificity. For example, do child workers in related jobs or industries have similar exposures? Do children in the same job have exposures similar but not identical to those listed?

Input and output requirements

The second component of the system's structure is diagnostic-specific: current and past symptoms, selected physical examination findings, radiographic findings. More specialized tests may be necessary in selected cases (which may be relevant but not generally available, for example, enzyme levels, blood-gas analysis, diffusing capacity, lung volumes, or other highly specific tests such as *in vitro* induced stimulation or specific antigen testing). In addition, information on personal risk factors such as a history of smoking and alcohol consumption (particularly in adolescence), allergic tendencies, and family history, would be necessary.

A detailed history of the individual industries where the child has worked and types of jobs or tasks developed is necessary. The materials used by the child or by the adjacent co-workers may be considered. Environmental factors are also relevant, including those cases in which mitigating factors were put in place such as respirators, industrial ventilation, work-practice modifications or other protective measures.

The type of agent or agents likely to have produced the disease should also be included, assigning a confidence factor (CF) for such associations. It should also describe which work or tasks are likely to be associated with the exposure and, if possible, the magnitude of the exposure. Finally the expert system should provide the user with a description of the rationale for reaching its conclusions.

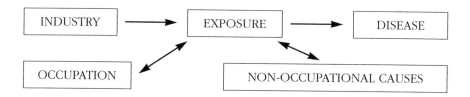

Algorithm

The third component of the database is a formal algorithm for establishing diagnosis using the data obtained from the individual worker and information from the knowledge database structure.

Specification of uncertainties and recognition of diagnostic "biases"

Each step of the process may be associated with uncertainties or incomplete data. The fourth structural component is a system to deal with uncertain data. A confidence factor is used to express belief in a certain statement, using a scale of 0 to 100 (no certainty to absolute certainty). The CF may express uncertainty of 2 types: about the knowledge (e.g. silica causes cancer is less certain than asbestos causes cancer); and uncertainty about data in case-specific information (e.g. the radiologist is 50 per cent certain that the radiograph is abnormal).

The following tables show examples of general categories of information concerning diseases (table A) and job exposures (table B).

The availability of this type of database system would facilitate the training of health personnel in occupational health aspects. Exposure information may lead to medical diagnosis and thereby encourage appropriate clinical referral. At the same time medical diagnosis could benefit from accurate and detailed exposure information. Some health professionals such as a hygienist may have particular knowledge about the relationship of a type of work to an exposure, but many lack broad knowledge about links between exposure and disease diagnosis, which is the field of competence of a clinical toxicologist. On the other hand, many specialist physicians have particular expertise in the relationship between signs and symptoms and the presence of a disease, but may lack broad knowledge about work-exposure relationships, particularly when mitigating factors have to be considered (industrial ventilation, respiratory use, etc.). It may also be useful to ascertain their personal diagnostic biases. Different biases may depend on the clinical context when physicians reach contradictory diagnostic conclusions using the same information.

Training of physicians, occupational health nurses, primary health care workers and community health workers in the diagnostic process itself can improve their abilities. In any case, a prerequisite is that health personnel systematically ask children about their activities at school, at work, at sport, etc. In the medical practice, it is widely known that it is necessary to stress the need to ask the patients about their profession. Many diagnoses are missed, and many epidemiological studies are weak, because there is not enough concern about the professional history of the patient. Similarly, concern about child labour by health professionals could dramatically increase if the right questions were asked. It would allow the real size and nature of the problem to be determined.

It has to be taken into consideration that this model focuses only upon diagnosis, and therefore the knowledge database structure excludes knowledge on prevention and regulation. Since the scope of the expert system is to identify exposure and possible occupational diseases of the individual specific child worker, the approach is clinically oriented. This means that it is designed to determine the exposure and disease resulting from a particular job; therefore, other complementary tools must be used in the development of an occupational health programme to reinforce the preventive and regulatory aspects.

TABLE A. DISEASE DATABASE

Occupation (job):

— Job title: general job category
— Type of activity: any tasks included in the job category
— Numeric code(s): range of codes from the dictionary of job titles
— Synonyms: synonymous terms
— Associated job(s): closely related jobs or tasks, closeness of association expressed by the association confidence factor (ACF)
— Confidence factor (CF): estimate of the certainty of the fact
— Source: textbooks, technical literature or other references for the fact confidence factor (CF)

Industry:

— Name: industry name
— Parent industry: the most general industry category of any occupation or job included in this industry
— Numeric code(s): codes from the standard industry classification (SIC)
— Synonyms: synonymous terms for this industry
— Asssociate industries: closely related industries, closeness of association expressed by ACF
— Source: textbooks, technical literature or other references for the fact confidence factor (CF)
— Confidence factor (CF): estimate of the certainty of the fact

Agent:

— Name: name of agent
— Parent agent: the more general class which includes this agent
— Agent derived: any agent included in this agent class
— Synonym: synonymous terms

Disease:

— Name: name of disease
— Parent: the more general disease class of which this is a member
— Derived: any disease(s) included within this one
— Synonym: synonymous terms

— Associate agents: closely related agents in terms of type of workers exposed and clinical effects), closeness of association expressed by an ACF

— Type of agent: physical state of agent (dust, mist, fume, etc.)

— Contaminants: agents which may contaminate this agent, frequency and level expressed by ACF

— Source: textbooks, technical literature or other references for the fact confidence factor (CF)

— Confidence factor (CF): estimate of the certainty of the fact of any occupational exposure

— Associate non-occupational diseases: endemic disease which can have synergistic effects (e.g. malnutrition, vitamin deficiencies)

— Smoking effects: to what extent does smoking cigarettes cause/contribute to the disease?

— Alcohol and drug effects: to what extent does alcohol and drug consumption cause/contribute to the disease?

— Age effect: direction and magnitude of age effect on disease likelihood

— Associate disease(s): disease(s) which appear(s) similar clinically

— Nonoccupational percentage: overall likelihood that the disease occurs in the absence of any occupational exposure

— Associate non-occupational disease(s): endemic disease which can have synergistic effects (e.g. malnutrition, vitamin deficiencies)

— Smoking effects: to what extent does smoking cigarettes cause/contribute to the disease?

— Alcohol and drug effects: to what extent does alcohol and drug consumption cause/contribute to the disease?

— Age effect: direction and magnitude of age effect on disease likelihood

— Duration: typical duration of disease

— Epidemiologic model: (D-T-T-L):

* dose: relationship of dose to disease likelihood (e.g. linear, exponential)

* time: typical length of exposure necessary to produce disease

* threshold: whether there is an exposure threshold for producing the disease

* latency: typical delay (if any) between onset of exposure and of disease

— Source: textbooks, technical literature or other references for the fact confidence factor (CF)

— Confidence factor (CF): estimate of the certainty of the fact

— Clinical characteristics: radiographic examinations, symptoms described as nature, direction and frequency; physical examinations, pulmonary function tests, other specific tests

TABLE B. JOB-EXPOSURE DATABASE

- Job exposure (JE): describes a particular exposure involved in a particular job
- Job: work involved in the JE pair
- Agent: agent involved in the JE pair
- Agent specificity: degree to which the relationship is highly specific for the particular agent, rather than possibly being relevant to associate jobs
- Frequency: proportion of workers in the job category who have the exposure
- Source: textbooks, technical literature or other references for the fact confidence factor (CF)
- Confidence factor (CF): estimate of the certainty of the fact
- Exposure disease (ED): describes a particular agent causing a particular disease
- Exposure: the particular agent involved
- Disease: the particular disease involved
- Exposure specificity: the degree to which the exposure-disease relationship may be generalized
- Frequency: proportion of exposed workers who develop the disease
- Potency: level of exposure necessary to produce the disease
- Source: textbooks, technical literature or other references for the fact confidence factor (CF)
- Confidence factor (CF): estimate of the certainty of the fact

NOTE

[1] Harber et al., 1991; Hayes-Roth et al., 1983.

Annex V

Sentinel Health Event (occupational)[1]

The successful control of occupational-related diseases of working children depends on the recognition and diagnosis of cases by physicians and on the implementation of specific programmes on occupational health surveillance, prevention and control of occupational diseases, including rehabilitation.

A Sentinel Health Event (SHE) in occupational health could be defined as an unexpected disease, disability or untimely death which is occupation-related and whose occurrence may:

(a) provide the impetus for epidemiological or occupational health studies; and

(b) serve as a warning signal for control requirements, such as material substitution, engineering control, personal protection or medical care.

For the implementation of a SHE system, it would be necessary to establish a list of SHEs obtained from surveys, health history forms, technical literature and epidemiological data (see table 6 for a model health history form, see also Part II, section 4: Identification and use of sources of information). This list should meet three criteria:

(a) documentation of associated agents;

(b) documentation of involved industries; and

(c) documentation of involved occupations or activities.

It should also be possible to codify the disease, health impairment or health condition within the framework of an international classification of occupational diseases, or a national adaptation of it, according to local practice (e.g. respiratory diseases).

In any case, it is important to take into consideration both occupational and non-occupational factors in the preparation and analysis of the medical history of the child.

The creation of such a system will allow the elaboration of a "core list" for occupational diseases associated with child labour or a priority list of prohibited activities for children (see tables 2 and 4), which could be developed and improved with this data.

The following is an example of a model table to present the SHE system graphically. It should include two broad categories of occupational diseases:

(1) the first group would include those diseases or health conditions which, because of their nature, are occupation-related, therefore they would not occur in the absence of an occupational exposure to the inciting agent (e.g. byssinosis);

(2) the second group would include those diseases or health conditions which may or may not be occupation-related (such as leukaemia or certain neuropathies).

The table should also indicate whether or not the disease, the disability or death can be controlled by prevention and/or treatment.

This table could be used as a surveillance tool by health personnel and medical doctors dealing with working children. The study of these events may indicate where follow-up is necessary. By scanning the table, the industry/occupation of the patient and the associated agent can be easily identified, thereby recognizing the occupational diseases in child patients and identifying the kinds of illness that are likely to be present when dealing with working children as patients. It is also a tool for researchers, as it provides a framework upon which to build. Conceiving the table as a periodically updated compendium of occupation-related diseases, it can provide an insight for priority-setting and decision-making on occupational safety and health research and action programmes for working children.

Previous attempts have been made to create mobility-based occupational health surveillance networks and to identify cases of high interest to follow-up.[2] However, these efforts have not always succeeded, because it is difficult to make a distinction between occupational and non-occupational factors, as in most cases the medical history is not available, even for adult workers. In the case of death certificates where exposure data are impossible to obtain, this table does have some limitations. In these cases exposure needs to be inferred from the deceased's last occupation. The occupation of the deceased may be recorded, or the death certificate may occasionally indicate a possible association between the cause of death and the employment history (but most probably not for child labourers). However, using death certificates as sources of information for an occupational surveillance system is not practical. Such a method would depend on the national system for the recording of data and hospital record-keeping, which often provide no record of the industry or occupation of the deceased, particularly in the case of a child or an adolescent.

Limitations due to the latency of certain health impairments can also be expected. An example is in the case of lung cancer in adult workers because, if cancer is discovered, the original environment in which the exposure took place may have changed. The problem may be even greater for young workers with a past history of child labour and high mobility between occupations and therefore exposures.

Model table:

Classification code no.	Health condition	A	B	C	Industry occupational activity	Agent
089	allergic dermatitis (o)	P,T	P,T	—	leather tanning	carbon disulphide

A = unnecessary disease
B = unnecessary disability
C = unnecessary death
(o) = when an occupational exposure can be established
P = prevention
T = treatment
Classification code no. = according to the list of occupational diseases chosen as "core list"

Accurate recording of occupational experience should be included on death certificates and on medical and hospital records, if the prevention, treatment and management of occupational diseases of children and youth is to be effective, and should be developed at the national level. Cooperation may be arranged between hospital administration and staff to attempt to obtain this type of information from hospital discharge records.

NOTES
    [1] Rustein et al., 1983.
    [2] Special issue of *American Journal of Industrial Medicine*, Sep. 1993, containing articles cited in the bibliography including Barbaro, Brooks, Landrigan, Lemen, Kinney, Wilks and others.

Bibliography

Alleyne, G.A.O., et al. 1977. "The effects of PEM in growth", in *Protein energy malnutrition* (London, Edward Arnold).

American Journal of Industrial Medicine. 1993. "Child labor: Health hazards and remedies" (New York, Wiley-Liss, Inc.), Vol. 24, No. 3, Sep.

Amin-Zaki, L., et al. 1976. "Perinatal methyl mercury poisoning in Iraq", in *American Journal of the Disabled Child*, No. 130.

Anti-Slavery Society. 1978. *Child labour in Morocco's carpet industry* (London).

—.1988. *A pattern of slavery: India's carpet boys* (London), Report No. 9.

Ard-am, O.; Sethaput, C. (eds.). 1994. *Child prostitution in Thailand: A documentary analysis and estimation of the number of child prostitutes* (Bangkok, Institute for Population and Social Research, Mahidol University).

Ashagrie, K. 1993. "Statistics on child labour: A brief report", in *Bulletin of Labour Statistics* (Geneva, ILO).

Azevedo, B.S., et al. 1993. "Diarrhoea and growth among children under 18 months of age in Rio de Janeiro", in *Bulletin of PAHO* (Washington, DC), Vol. 27, No. 2.

Barbaro, F.J. 1993. "Child labour legislation in New York State: A 1990s update", in *American Journal of Industrial Medicine* (New York, Wiley-Liss, Inc.), Vol. 24, No. 3, Sep.

Barry, P.S.I. 1975. "A comparison of concentrations of lead in human tissues", in *British Journal of Industrial Medicine* (London), No. 32.

Bellinger, D. 1991. "Children exposed to lead: Clear and present danger, Environmental health special report", in *Medical and Health Annual Britannica* (London), Nov.

Bellville, R., et al. 1993. "Occupational injuries among working adolescents in New York State", in *Journal of the American Medical Association* (New York), Vol. 269, No. 21, June.

Bennett, F. 1991. "Effectiveness of developmental intervention in the first five years of life", in *Pediatric Clinics of North America* (Philadelphia), No. 38.

Bequele, A.; Boyden, J. (eds.). 1988. *Combating child labour* (Geneva, ILO).

Berger, L.R., et al. 1991. "Medical aspects of child labor in developing countries", in *American Journal of Industrial Medicine* (New York, Wiley-Liss, Inc.), Vol. 19, Mar.

Bouldring, E. 1979. *Children's rights and the wheel of life* (New Brunswick, Transaction Books and New York, United Nations).

Brooks, D.R., et al. 1993. "Work-related injuries among Massachusetts children: A study based on emergency department data", in *American Journal of Industrial Medicine* (New York, Wiley-Liss, Inc.), Vol. 24, No. 3, Sep.

Burkhart, G., et al. 1993. "Job tasks, potential exposures, and health risks of laborers employed in the construction industry", in *American Journal of Industrial Medicine* (New York, Wiley-Liss, Inc.), Vol. 24.

Burra, N. 1988. "Exploitation of children in the Jaipur gem industry", in *Economic and Political Weekly* (New Delhi), Vol. XXIII, Nos. 1 and 2, Jan.

Challis, J.; Elliman, D. (eds.). 1988. *Child workers today* (London, Anti-Slavery Society).

Cogbill, T.H., et al. 1985. "Farm accidents in children", in *Pediatrics* (Elk Grove Village, Illinois), Vol. 76, No. 4, Oct.

Cusminsky, M., et al. 1986. *Manual de crecimiento y desarrollo*, Organización Panamericana de la Salud, (Serie Palex, No. 7) (Washington, DC, OPS-PAHO).

Das, P.K., et al. 1992. "An occupational health programme for adults and children in the carpet-weaving industry, Mirzapur, India: A case study in the informal sector", in *Social Science and Medicine* (London, Pergamon Press), Vol. 35, No. 10.

Deeds, S.G.; Gunatilake, S. 1989. "Behavioural change strategies to enhance child survival", in *HYGIE* (Paris), Vol. VIII, No. 4.

Department of Labor and Employment (Philippines)/ILO. 1987. *A pilot project on child scavengers in Metro Manila* (Manila, Doc. PHI/87/M01/NET).

Doyle, Y; Conroy, R. 1989. "Childhood farm accidents: A continuing cause for concern", in *Journal of Social and Occupational Medicine* (London), No. 39.

ECPAT. 1995. "End of child prostitution in Asian tourism: An introduction to ECPAT" (Bangkok), mimeo.

Feingold, E.; Wasser, J. 1994. "Walk-through surveys for child labor", in *American Journal of Industrial Medicine* (New York, Wiley-Liss, Inc.), Vol. 26.

Fescina R.H., et al. 1995. "Fetal and child growth and development", in H.M. Wallace (ed.): *Health care of women and children in developing countries*, 2nd edition (Oakland, California, Third Party Publishing Company).

Forastieri, V. 1995. "Child and adolescent labor", in H.M. Wallace (ed.): *Health care of women and children in developing countries*, 2nd edition (Oakland, California, Third Party Publishing Company).

Forssman, S.; Coppée, G.H. 1984. *Occupational health problems of young workers* (Geneva, ILO). Occupational Safety and Health Series No. 26.

Goonesekere, S.W.E. 1993. *Child labour in Sri Lanka* (Geneva, ILO).

Gorstein, J., et al. 1994. "Issues in the assessment of nutritional status using anthropometry", in *Bulletin of the World Health Organization* (Geneva, WHO). No. 72(2).

Green, L.W.; McAlister, A.L. 1984. "Macro intervention to support health behavior: Some theoretical perspectives and practical reflections", in *Health Education Quarterly* (New York, John Wiley). Vol. 2, No. 3.

Guerra de Macedo, C. 1988. *Infant mortality in the Americas* (Washington, DC, Pan American Health Organization).

Gupta, B.N., et al. 1984. *A study of morbidity and socio-economic conditions of workers in the glass bangle industry* (Lucknow, India, Industrial Toxicology Research Centre).

Gupta, K. 1992. *Model workshop on child labour for factory inspectors and labour inspectors* (Geneva, ILO/IPEC), internal document.

Gupta, M. 1989. *Child labour in hazardous work in India: Situation and policy experience* (Geneva, ILO), unpublished study.

Gutloff, K. 1990. *Caution: Children at work* (Washington, DC, National Child Labour Committee Union), Summer.

Harber, P., et al. 1991. "The structure of expert diagnostic knowledge in occupational medicine", in *American Journal of Industrial Medicine* (New York, Wiley-Liss, Inc.), Vol. 19, Mar.

Hawes, H. 1988. *Child to child: Another path to learning* (Hamburg, Germany, UNESCO Institute for Education). UIE Monographs, No. 13.

Hayes-Roth, F., et al. 1983. *Building expert systems* (New York, Addison Wesley).

Hussain, A. 1992. *Child workers in construction and related industries in Pakistan* (Geneva, ILO), unpublished study.

ILO. 1981. *General survey by the Committee of Experts on the Application of Conventions and Recommendations concerning Minimum Age*, International Labour Conference, 67th Session (Geneva).

—. 1983. *Child labour*, Extract from the Report of the Director-General to the International Labour Conference, 69th Session (Geneva).

—. 1986. *Survey of working conditions of child workers in the provinces of Kanchanaburi, Ratchaburi and Samut Songkhram* (Bangkok), RICE Project Technical Report Doc. RICE/UNDP/ILO/THA/86/012.

—. 1987. *ILO pilot project on child scavengers in Metro Manila* (Geneva). Doc. PHI/87/M01/NET.

—. 1988. "The emerging response to child labour", in *Conditions of Work Digest* (Geneva), Vol. 7, No. 1.

—. 1989a. *Still so far to go: Child labour in the world today*, Special report on the occasion of the Tenth Anniversary of the International Year of the Child (Geneva).

—. 1989b. *Encyclopaedia of Occupational Health and Safety*, 3rd (revised) ed. (Geneva).

—. 1990a. *Report of the Committee of Experts on the Application of Conventions and Recommendations, General report and observations concerning particular countries*, International Labour Conference, 77th Session, Report III (Part 4A) (Geneva).

—. 1990b. *Child care: Annotated bibliography on child labour* (Geneva), International Labour Bibliography No. 5.

—. 1991a. "Child labour: Law and practice", in *Conditions of Work Digest* (Geneva), Vol. 10, No. 1.

—. 1991b. *Occupational lung diseases: Prevention and control* (Geneva), Occupational Safety and Health Series No. 67.

—. 1991c. *Report of the Director-General*, Eleventh Asia-Pacific Regional Conference (Bangkok), Nov./Dec.

—. 1995. *Child Labour.* Governing Body Paper, 264th Session (Geneva), Nov., Doc. GB264/ESP/1.

—. 1996a. *Child labour surveys: Results of methodological experiments in four countries 1992-1993* (Geneva).

—. 1996b. *Child labour: Targeting the intolerable* (Geneva).

ILO-CIS. 1989. *Bibliography, laws, regulations and directives from the CISDOC Database* (Geneva).

IPCS: International Programme on Chemical Safety. 1986. "Principles for evaluating health risks from chemicals during infancy and early childhood: The need for a special approach", in *Environmental Health Criteria* (Geneva, ILO/UNEP/WHO), No. 59.

—. 1995. *Basic analytical toxicology* (Geneva, ILO/UNEP/WHO).

International Catholic Child Bureau. 1991. *The sexual exploitation of children: Field responses* (Geneva).

Janz, N.K.; Becker, M.H. 1984. "The health belief model: A decade later", in *Health Education Quarterly* (New York, John Wiley), Vol. 11, No. 1.

Jeyaratnam, J. 1985. "1984 and occupational health in developing countries", in *Scandinavian Journal on Working Environment and Health* (Helsinki), No. II.

—. (ed.) 1992. *Occupational health in developing countries* (Oxford, Oxford University Press).

—; Chia, K.S. (eds.) 1994. *Occupational health in national development* (Singapore, World Scientific Publishing Co.).

Khan, T.M.; Shah S.H. 1991. *A survey of children in the brick kilns of Peshawar* (Peshawar, NWFP, Pakistan Paediatric Association), mimeo.

Kinney, J.A. 1993. "Health hazards to children in the service industry", in *American Journal of Industrial Medicine* (New York, Wiley-Liss, Inc.), Vol. 24, No. 3, Sep.

Kneel, F.M. 1995. *Young workers, street life and gender: The effect of education and work experience on earnings in Colombia* (Cambridge, Massachusetts, Harvard University), doctoral thesis.

Kothari, S. 1983. "There's blood on those matchsticks: Child labour in Sirakasi, Bombay", in *Economic and Political Weekly* (Bombay), Vol. XVIII, No. 27, July.

Kumar L., et al. 1990. "Acute respiratory infections", in H.M. Wallace (ed.): *Health care of women and children in developing countries* (Oakland, California, Third Party Publishing Company).

Landrigan, P.J. 1993a. "Child labor: A re-emerging threat", in *American Journal of Industrial Medicine* (New York, Wiley-Liss, Inc.), Vol. 24, No. 3, Sep.

—. 1993b. "Child labor: Health hazards and remedies", in *American Journal of Industrial Medicine* (New York, Wiley-Liss, Inc.), Vol. 24, No. 3, Sep.

Lemen, R.A., et al. 1993. "Children at work: Prevention of occupational injury and disease", in *American Journal of Industrial Medicine* (New York, Wiley-Liss, Inc.), Vol. 24, No. 3, Sep.

Levy, B.; Wegman, D. (eds.). 1988. *Occupational health: Recognizing and preventing work-related diseases* (Boston, Massachusetts, Little, Brown and Company).

Lukindo, J.K. 1992. *Proposed model workshop on child labour for labour and factory inspectors in East African countries* (Geneva, ILO/IPEC), internal document.

Mancian, M,; Romer, C.J. (eds.). 1991. *Accidents in childhood and adolescence: The role of research* (Geneva, WHO).

Manereffe, C. 1993. "The violent family: Balancing between support and control" in *Archive of Public Health* (Brussels), No. 51.

Mattoo, G.M., et al. 1986. "Health status of school-age children employed in carpet weaving in Ganderbal Block", in *British Journal of Industrial Medicine* (London), No. 43.

McCunney, J.R. 1994. *A practical approach to occupational and environmental medicine*, 2nd ed. (Boston, Massachusetts, Little, Brown and Company).

McGuigan, M.A. 1994. "Exposure of working children to toxic substances: Its medical control", in *International child health: A digest of current information* (Geneva, International Paediatric Association in collaboration with the WHO and UNICEF), Vol. V, No. 2, Apr.

Mitra, S. 1991. *A study of health conditions of the child labourers in a small-scale industry in Calcutta* (Calcutta, All India Institute of Hygiene and Public Health, University of Calcutta), doctoral thesis.

Morehead, C. 1987. *School age children in Britain today* (London, Anti-Slavery Society), Report No. 8.

Morley, D. 1983. *Practising health for all* (Oxford, Oxford University Press).

Mouli, V.C. 1991. "Crash course in survival skills: Reaching street children in Zambia", in *AIDS health promotion exchange* (Geneva, WHO).

Myers, W.E. 1989. "Urban working children: A compilation of four surveys from South America", in *International Labour Review* (Geneva, ILO), Vol. 128, No. 3.

Nagi, M. H. 1972. "Child labor in rural Egypt", in *Rural Sociology Review* (Weavenhall, Pennsylvania), Vol. 37, No. 4, Dec.

Narang Spaak, A. 1990. *Working with deprived children in India (mobile crèches)* (New Delhi, ILO), unpublished report.

National Committee for Injury Prevention and Control. 1989. "Injury prevention: Meeting the challenge", supplement to the *American Journal for Preventive Medicine* (New York, Oxford University Press), Vol. 5, No. 3.

New York State Labor Legacy Committee. 1989. *The working teenager* (Albany, New York).

Pakistan Paediatric Association. 1991. *Proceedings of the First National Conference on Child Abuse in Pakistan* (Peshawar, NWFP), Oct.

Pill, D., et al. (eds.). 1981. *Child labour: A threat to health and development* (Geneva, WHO).

Pollack, S.H., et al. 1990a. "Pesticide exposure and working conditions among migrant farm worker children in western New York State" (New York). Lecture presented to the American Public Health Association annual meeting, New York, Oct.

—, et al. 1990b. "Child labor in 1990: Prevalence and health hazards", in *Annual Review of Public Health* (New York, Annual Review Inc.), Vol. 11.

Puffer, R.; Serrano, C.V. 1973. "Pattern of mortality in childhood", in *Scientific Publications* (Washington, DC, Pan American Health Organization), No. 262.

—, et al. 1989. "Thermal stress and physiological strain of children exposed to hot environments in a glass bangle factory", in *European Journal of Applied Physiology* (Berlin, Springer-Verlag), No. 59.

Rastogi, S.K., et al. 1984. *A study of morbidity and socio-economic conditions of workers in the glass bangle industry* (Industrial Toxicology Research Centre, Lucknow, India).

Reed, M.D.; Besunder, J.B. 1989. "Developmental pharmacology: Ontogenic basis of drug disposition", in *Paediatric Clinics of North America* (Philadelphia), No. 36.

Rialp, V. 1993. *Children in hazardous work in the Philippines* (Geneva, ILO).

Ribeiro Galasso, L. 1989. *Child labour in hazardous employment: Inspection and enforcement in São Paulo, Brazil* (São Paulo, ILO/CLASET), unpublished report.

Richter, E.D.; Jacobs, J. 1991. "Work injuries and exposures in children and young adults: Review and recommendations for action", in *American Journal of Industrial Medicine* (New York, Wiley-Liss, Inc.), Vol. 19, Mar.

Rosario, A. 1988. "Ragpicking and ragpickers: Education and development scheme in Bangalore City", in *Prevention and protection of working children and abandoned children: Country reports and case studies* (Bangkok), Second Asian Regional Conference on Child Abuse and Neglect, Bangkok, 8-13 Feb.

Rustein, D.D., et al. 1983. "Sentinel Health Events (occupational): A basis for physician recognition and public health surveillance", in *American Journal of Public Health* (Washington, DC), Vol. 73, No. 9, Sep.

Satyanarayana, K., et al. 1979. "Nutritional deprivation in childhood and the body size activity and physical work capacity of young boys", in *American Journal of Clinical Nutrition* (Bethesda, Maryland), No. 32.

—. 1986. "Effect of early childhood under-nutrition and child labour on growth and adult nutritional status of rural Indian boys around Hyderabad", in *Human Nutrition: Clinical Nutrition* (Westport, Connecticut), No. 40.

Schober, S.E., et al. 1988. "Work-related injuries in minors", in *American Journal of Industrial Medicine* (New York, Wiley-Liss, Inc.), Vol. 14.

Senanayake, N.; Román, G.C. 1993. "Epidemiology of epilepsy in developing countries", in *Bulletin of the World Health Organization* (Geneva, WHO), Vol. 71, No. 2.

Shah, P.M.; Cantwell, N. (eds.). 1985. *Child labour: A threat to health and development*, 2nd (revised) ed. (Geneva, Defence for Children International).

Simonson, J.R. 1993. "Congressional approaches toward remedies to problems of child labor", in *American Journal of Industrial Medicine* (New York, Wiley-Liss, Inc.), Vol. 24, No. 3, Sep.

Snyder, J.D.; Merson, M.H. 1982. "The magnitude of the global problem of acute surveillance data", in *Bulletin of the World Health Organization* (Geneva, WHO), Vol. 60.

Srivastava, A.K.; Gupta, B.N. 1987. *Report on child labour* (Lucknow, India, Industrial Toxicology Research Centre).

Suruda, A.; Halperin, W. 1991. "Work-related deaths in children", in *American Journal of Industrial Medicine* (New York, Wiley-Liss, Inc.), Vol 19.

Tanner, J.M. 1961. *Education and physical growth* (Oxford, Blackwell Scientific Publications).

—, et al. 1966. "Standards from birth to maturity for height, weight, height velocity and weight velocity in British children (part II)", in *Archive of Disabled Childhood* (London), No. 41.

Taylor, R.B. 1973. *Sweat shops in the sun: Child labour in the farm* (Boston, Massachusetts, Beacon Press).

Terra, J.P. 1988. "Estado nutricional y desarrollo psicomotor en los niños de las familias pobres", in *Cuadernos del CLAEH* (Montevideo, Banda Oriental, CLAEH-UNICEF), No. 47.

Trattner, W.I. 1970. *Crusade for the children: A history of the National Child Labor Committee and child labor reform in America* (Chicago, Quadrangle).

UNICEF. 1982. "The participatory imperative in primary health care", in *Assignment: Children* (Geneva), Nos. 59/60.

—. 1988. *The State of the World's Children 1988* (New York, Oxford University Press).

—. 1989. *The State of the World's Children 1989* (New York, Oxford University Press).

—. 1990. "Le travail des enfants", in *Fiche pédagogique* (Paris), No. 2.

—. 1991. *Child labour in Egypt* (Cairo, National Centre for Social and Criminological Research in collaboration with UNICEF and Shorouk Press, 1991).

—. 1992. *State of the World's Children 1989 to 1991* (Oxford, Oxford University Press).

United Kingdom Department of Health and Social Security. 1980. *Lead and Health*, Report of a DHSS working party on lead in the environment (London, Her Majesty's Stationery Office).

United Nations. 1987. *First Report on the World Nutrition Situation* (New York).

United States General Accounting Office. 1990. *Increases in detected child labor violations throughout the United States* (Washington, DC), Doc. GAO/HRD 90-116, Apr.

Valcarenghi, M. 1981. *Child labour in Italy* (London, Anti-Slavery Society), Report No. 5.

Wallace, H.M. 1990. "Handicapped children and youth in developing countries", in H.M. Wallace (ed.): *Health care of women and children in developing countries* (Oakland, California, Third Party Publishing Company).

Wanjiku Kaime-Atterhög, et al. 1994. *Child prostitution in Thailand: A documentary assessment* (Bangkok, Institute of Population and Social Research, Mahidol University).

Weisburger, J.H., et al. 1966. "Liver cancer: Neonatal oestrogen enhances induction by carcinogens", in *Science* (Washington, DC), No. 154.

Wester, R.C.; Maibach, H.I. 1982. "Percutaneous absoption: Neonate compared to the adult", in V.R. Hunt et al. (eds.): *Environmental factors in human growth and development* (New York, Cold Spring Harbor Laboratory), Banbury Report No. 2.

White, R.F., et al. 1993. "Residual cognitive deficits 50 years after lead poisoning during childhood", in *British Journal of Industrial Medicine* (London), No. 50.

WHO. 1976. *Expert Committee on Maternal and Child Health* (Geneva), Technical Report Series No. 600.

—. 1981. *Child labour: A threat to health and development* (Geneva).

—. 1983. *Report on apartheid and health* (Geneva).

—. 1984. *The organization and evaluation of workshop training for action-research in child labour and health* (Bombay, EMR/SEAR/WPR), Report of a WHO inter-regional workshop on research methodology and techniques to study the health problems of working children, 21-26 May.

—. 1985. *Prototype home-based mother's record — guidelines for use and adaptation in maternal and child health/family planning programmes* (Doc. MCH/85.13) (Geneva).

—. 1986a. *Early detection of occupational diseases* (Geneva).

—. 1986b. *Epidemiology of occupational health* (Copenhagen, WHO Regional Publications), European Series No. 20.

—. 1987a. *Children at work: Special health risks* (Geneva), Technical Report Series No. 756.

—. 1987b. *Nutrition in preventive medicine* (Geneva), Monograph Series No. 62.

—. 1987c. *Measurement in health promotion and protection* (Copenhagen, WHO Regional Publications), European Series No. 22.

—. 1987d. *Evaluation of the strategy for health for all by the year 2000* (Geneva), Seventh Report on the World Health Situation, Vol. I.

—. 1988. *Training manual on research and action methodologies and techniques concerning health of working children, revised version* (Geneva).

—. 1989. "The health of youth", Background document for technical discussion (Geneva), May.

—. 1993a. "Epilepsy in developing countries", in *Bulletin of the World Health Organization* (Geneva), Vol. 71.

—. 1993b. *A one way street? Report on Phase I of Street Children Project*, (Geneva), Doc. WHO/PSA/93.7.

William, N.R. (ed.). 1986. *Environmental and occupational medicine* (Boston, Massachusetts, Little, Brown and Company).

Wilks, V.A. 1993. "Health hazards to children in agriculture", in *American Journal of Industrial Medicine* (New York, Wiley-Liss, Inc.), Vol. 24, No. 3, Sep.

World Bank. 1991. *World Development Report 1991* (New York and Oxford, Oxford University Press).

—. 1993. *World Development Report 1993* (New York and Oxford, Oxford University Press).